SHAPE IT! 2

WORKBOOK
WITH EBOOK
Annie Cornford

CAMBRIDGE
UNIVERSITY PRESS

Shaftesbury Road, Cambridge CB2 8EA, United Kingdom

One Liberty Plaza, 20th Floor, New York, NY 10006, USA

477 Williamstown Road, Port Melbourne, VIC 3207, Australia

314–321, 3rd Floor, Plot 3, Splendor Forum, Jasola District Centre, New Delhi – 110025, India

103 Penang Road, #05–06/07, Visioncrest Commercial, Singapore 238467

Avenida Paulista, 807 conjunto 2315, 01311–915, São Paulo, Brazil

Torre de los Parques, Colonia Tlacoquemécatl del Valle, Mexico City CP 03200, Mexico

Cambridge University Press & Assessment is a department of the University of Cambridge.

We share the University's mission to contribute to society through the pursuit of education, learning and research at the highest international levels of excellence.

www.cambridge.org
Information on this title: www.cambridge.org/9781009043021

© Cambridge University Press & Assessment 2020

First published 2020

20 19 18 17 16 15 14

Printed in Poland by Opolgraf

A catalogue record for this publication is available from the British Library

ISBN   978-1-009-04302-1   Shape It! Workbook with eBook Level 2
ISBN   978-1-009-04352-6   Own it! Workbook with eBook Level 2

Additional resources for this publication at www.cambridge.org/shapeit

Cambridge University Press & Assessment has no responsibility for the persistence or accuracy of URLs for external or third-party internet websites referred to in this publication and does not guarantee that any content on such websites is, or will remain, accurate or appropriate. Information regarding prices, travel timetables, and other factual information given in this work is correct at the time of first printing but Cambridge University Press & Assessment does not guarantee the accuracy of such information thereafter.

CONTENTS

Starter Unit Welcome! p4

Unit 1 What are you watching? p8

Unit 2 How was the past different? p16

Unit 3 What do stories teach us? p24

Unit 4 What do you value most? p32

Unit 5 What is your dream house? p40

Unit 6 How can I stay safe? p48

Unit 7 Are you connected? p56

Unit 8 What is success? p64

Unit 9 How do you express yourself? p72

Exam Tips & Practice p80

Grammar Reference & Practice p86

Language Bank p106

Irregular Verbs p111

STARTER

Welcome!

VOCABULARY AND READING
Free Time and Hobbies

1 ☆ **Match six of the phrases in the box with the photos.**

1 chat online   2 download songs and listen to music
3 go shopping   4 go for a bike ride   5 hang out with
friends   6 make cookies   7 make videos   8 play an
instrument   9 read books   10 read magazines
11 take photos   12 write a blog

Sports

2 ☆ **Put the letters in the correct order to make sports words. The first letter is given.**

1 b e a t l n n e t s i   t̲a̲b̲l̲e̲ ̲t̲e̲n̲n̲i̲s̲
2 b r g y u   r_____
3 k t a r c n d a e i l f d   t_____
4 i s a g i l n   s_____
5 c e h o k y   h_____
6 n m a y s g t s c i   g_____
7 b y v l e l a l o l   v_____
8 s a a b b l l t e k   b_____
9 w s i g m i m n   s_____
10 s w n f i u r n g d i   w_____

A Blog Post

3 ☆ **Read Pablo's blog post. What is his best friend's favorite activity?** _____

| Home | News | **Blog** | Lifestyle | | Q |

My Friends and Their Hobbies

Hi there, Pablo here! Today my blog
is about two of my friends and their
hobbies.

Carla lives in an apartment in our
building. We go to the same school,
but we aren't in the same class.
Carla loves riding her bike, so she
usually cycles to school. I don't cycle
when the weather's bad, but I like to
ride my bike with her in the summer.
Carla also plays hockey and does
gymnastics – she's very athletic!

Nico is my best friend – he's Italian.
He speaks Italian at home with his
family, but he doesn't speak Italian
with me. He plays volleyball on
our school team on Wednesday
afternoons and Saturday mornings.
On Sundays, we often do his favorite
free-time activity: making pizza! His
dad's a chef in a pizzeria, so Nico
knows a lot about pizza – and I like
eating pizza a lot!

4 ☆☆ **Read the blog again. Circle the correct options.**
1 Carla and Pablo *go* / *don't go* to the same school.
2 Pablo *cycles* / *doesn't cycle* to school every day.
3 Carla's very *good* / *bad* at sports.
4 Pablo's best friend *speaks* / *doesn't speak* Italian.
5 Pablo likes *making* / *eating* pizza.

Explore It! 🖱

Guess the correct answer.

Marathon runners often lose height when they
run a race. On average, a marathon runner is
1 cm / 5 cm / 10 cm shorter at the end of a race.

**Find another interesting fact about running.
Write a question and send it to a classmate in an
email, or ask them in the next class.**

GRAMMAR IN ACTION AND VOCABULARY

Simple Present

1 ☆ **Complete the sentences with the simple present form of the verbs in the box.**

> go   make   ~~play~~   not see   write

1 Max ___plays___ computer games every day.
2 Lena's friend _____ to a different school.
3 We _____ our friends on Sunday evenings.
4 I _____ my blog two or three times a week.
5 Martha _____ videos of her pets.

2 ☆☆ **Write questions about Pablo's blog and answer them. Then check on page 4.**

1 when / Pablo / ride his bike with Carla ?

   When does Pablo ride his bike with Carla?
   Pablo rides his bike with Carla in the summer.

2 what sports / Carla / do ?

   _____
   _____

3 where / Nico's father / work ?

   _____
   _____

4 what / Nico / know a lot about ?

   _____
   _____

Adverbs of Frequency

3 ☆☆ **Put the words in the correct order to make sentences.**

1 computer / often / I / magazines / read / .

   I often read computer magazines.

2 never / hockey / Iris / late / practice / is / for / .

   _____

3 takes / photos / great / always / Paul / .

   _____

4 sometimes / next / Molly / to / friend / sits / her / .

   _____

5 music / you / listen / Do / to / usually / loud / ?

   _____

Personal Possessions

4 ☆☆ **Find the ten personal possessions in the photos in the wordsearch. Mark (✓) the photos when you find the words.**

T	N	O	H	M	C	H	S	A	L	J	N
A	Z	Q	S	O	I	B	C	D	S	G	H
B	U	R	R	N	O	A	L	H	S	S	J
L	Y	D	K	E	Y	S	H	E	F	C	H
E	F	M	W	Y	R	P	S	A	O	H	G
T	V	L	S	I	E	T	D	D	P	A	C
F	K	S	C	P	A	S	S	P	O	R	T
K	V	W	J	H	D	S	U	H	R	G	O
L	A	P	T	O	P	D	B	O	T	E	S
O	B	U	P	N	L	P	D	N	A	R	A
U	C	A	M	E	R	A	C	E	B	R	L
T	E	Y	N	J	A	N	W	S	L	E	G
D	S	K	L	H	Q	L	D	A	E	D	F
B	U	S	P	A	S	S	P	N	M	O	V

LISTENING AND GRAMMAR IN ACTION

A Conversation

🎧 **1** ⭐ **Listen and (circle) the correct option.**

S.01

Hannah meets Mrs. Hayes at the store / gym / bus stop.

🎧 **2** ⭐⭐ **Listen again. Mark (✓) the activities that Hannah and Joe do.**

S.01

	Gymnastics Class	Running Club	Photography Club	Play Video Games
Hannah	✓			
Joe	✗			

🎧 **3** ⭐⭐ **Listen again. Are the sentences T (true) or F (false)?**

S.01

1 Mrs. Hayes likes doing sports on the weekend. ___F___

2 Joe goes to a running club on Saturday evenings. ___

3 The gymnastics class is one and a half hours long. ___

4 The school's photography club is once a week. ___

5 Joe likes writing video games. ___

6 Hannah does her homework on the weekend. ___

Love, Like, Don't Mind, Hate + -ing

4 ⭐⭐ **Complete the sentences with the correct form of the verbs in the box.**

> ~~be~~   help   play   speak   use   write

1 Susie hates ___being___ late for class, so she always arrives early.

2 Harry doesn't mind _____ soccer, but it's not his favorite sport.

3 I love _____ English, so I often call my cousins in the U.S.A.

4 Do you like _____ headphones when you listen to music?

5 Bella loves _____ her blog. It's really good, and we all read it.

6 Good friends don't mind _____ you when you have a problem.

To Have

5 ⭐⭐ **Complete the questions and short answers with the correct form of to have.**

1 A ___Do___ you ___have___ your own computer?

  B Yes, ___I do___ .

2 A _____ Jack _____ his own keys?

  B Yes, _____ .

3 A _____ Enzo and Lou _____ a French mother?

  B No, _____ .

4 A _____ I _____ the right phone number for you?

  B No, _____ .

5 A _____ we _____ any math homework today?

  B Yes, _____ .

6 A _____ your mom _____ a new laptop?

  B Yes, _____ .

6 ⭐⭐ **(Circle) the correct options to complete the email.**

● ● ●

Dear Leo,

I ¹(have) / has some exciting news. We ² have / don't have new neighbors, and there's a girl named Jessica – she's my new friend. ³ Do we have / We have a lot in common? Yes, we ⁴ don't / do! She's my age and she ⁵ has / have long dark hair, just like me. She loves ⁶ listen / listening to music and singing, and she ⁷ has / doesn't have her own band – so cool! She ⁸ don't have / doesn't have any sisters or brothers, but I don't mind ⁹ to share / sharing my annoying little brothers with her! Jessica and I ¹⁰ love / hate hanging out together already!

See you soon!

Anita

WRITING
A Personal Profile

1 ⭐ **Read Bruna's profile of her brothers. When are they all free to hang out together?**

_____

| HOME | ABOUT ME | ARCHIVE | FOLLOW |

1 Hi! My name's Bruna, and this profile is about my two brothers. We're from São Paulo, in Brazil. My brothers are named Victor and Lucas. Victor's nine years old and Lucas is 12. I'm 14.

2 Lucas is crazy about soccer, like a lot of people in Brazil! He practices on Mondays, Wednesdays, Fridays, and Saturdays! He never minds getting home late because he just loves playing. Victor's favorite free-time activity is swimming. He has a great coach, and he gets up early for lessons with her in the pool at the gym.

3 Lucas and Victor also like playing table tennis, and we all love doing that together. We have a table tennis table in our garage, and we often play on Sundays when we're all free. I sometimes find Lucas annoying, but he's usually a lot of fun, and Victor is OK. Do you have brothers and sisters? What are they like?

2 ⭐⭐ **Read the profile again. Are the sentences _T_ (true) or _F_ (false)?**

1 Lucas and Victor have one sister. T

2 Lucas has soccer practice on the weekend. ___

3 Lucas never gets home late from practice. ___

4 Victor prefers table tennis to swimming. ___

5 Bruna doesn't play table tennis with her brothers. ___

3 ⭐⭐ **Read the profile again. <u>Underline</u> one example of …**

1 's for possession   3 commas in a list

2 's for _is_

4 ⭐⭐ **Rewrite the text with contractions, apostrophes, and commas in your notebook.**

My friend Mason has a big family. He has two brothers two sisters and 35 cousins. They all live on the same street! In Masons house, there are a lot of pets. They have two dogs three cats four rabbits and a parrot! They have a big house and a big yard, so there is lots of space!

PLAN

5 ⭐⭐ **Write a profile of a friend or a family member. Take notes for each paragraph.**

1 Their family and friends:

_____

_____

2 Their favorite free-time activity:
- what it is and where they do it
- how often they do it

_____

3 Other free-time activities:
- what they like doing on their own or with friends
- when and where they do the activities

_____

WRITE

6 ⭐⭐⭐ **Write your profile. Remember to include three paragraphs, the information in Exercise 5, the simple present, adverbs of frequency, _love_, etc. + _-ing_, and _to have_.**

CHECK

7 Do you …
- describe the family and friends of the person in your profile?
- explain their favorite free-time activity?
- say what else they like doing, and when?

1 What are you watching?

VOCABULARY
TV Shows

1 ⭐ **Complete the words with the missing vowels.**

1 str e a m i ng s e r i e s
2 sp _ _ rts sh _ w
3 d _ c _ m _ nt _ ry
4 dr _ m _
5 g _ m _ sh _ w
6 t _ lk sh _ w

7 s _ _ p _ p _ r _
8 th _ n _ ws
9 c _ m _ dy
10 c _ _ k _ ng sh _ w
11 c _ rt _ _ n
12 r _ _ l _ ty sh _ w

2 ⭐ (Circle) **the correct options.**

1 What is the first prize on the TV *drama* / (*game show*) this week?
2 Dan loves food, so he watches all the *sports* / *cooking* shows.
3 Adele is talking to some great guests on tonight's *soap opera* / *talk show*.
4 We always laugh a lot at the new *drama* / *comedy* on Channel 4 because it's really funny.
5 Sam watches *the news* / *a streaming series* to learn about world events.
6 Now they use computers to make *documentaries* / *cartoons*. They don't draw them by hand.

3 ⭐ **Match the definitions with TV shows from Exercise 1.**

1 a show about a subject, like history or nature. _documentary_
2 information about real world events. _____
3 information about tennis, soccer, basketball, etc.
   _____
4 an animated story, usually for younger people.
   _____
5 a show on which you answer questions and win prizes.
   _____
6 a show about real people in their ordinary lives.
   _____

4 ⭐⭐ **Complete the text about Elena's family with the words in the box.**

| comedies | cooking shows | ~~dramas~~ |
| soap operas | streaming series | talk shows |

My parents enjoy watching TV
¹ _dramas_ , especially when they are true stories from history. They both like
² _____ with famous chefs, too. My dad also enjoys
³ _____ on late-night TV. They make him laugh, but I don't think his favorite shows are funny at all! My mom watches ⁴ _____ with interesting celebrities talking about their latest movies, and I sometimes watch them with her. My grandma enjoys her favorite ⁵ _____ because she knows all the characters and is interested in their lives. I usually prefer
⁶ _____ to regular TV shows because I can watch them when I want to. I love that!

Explore It! 🖱

Guess the correct answer.
Blue Peter, the oldest children's TV show in the world, is about *40 / 60 / 80* years old.

Find another interesting fact about a TV show in your country. Write a question and send it to a classmate in an email, or ask them in the next class.

READING

Tweets

1 ⭐ Read the tweets. Which tweeter isn't very happy?

_____

2 ⭐⭐ Read the tweets again and check the meaning of these words in a dictionary. Then complete the sentences.

> billion   ~~competitor~~   fact   live   support

1 Amy's not a _competitor_. She's watching the event on TV today.

2 There's an interesting _____ about the number of people that watched the last Olympics.

3 More than 3 _____ people watch the World Cup Final on TV. That's more than 3,000 million people!

4 The game is _____ – all the action is happening now.

5 Which team on tonight's game show do you _____?

3 ⭐⭐ Read the tweets again and answer the questions.

1 At what time can people watch the UEFA Champions League Final live?
at eight o'clock

2 What doesn't Manny want to watch?
_____

3 Where is Amy today?
_____

4 What sport does Amy like playing?
_____

5 What can people watch on Channel 1 at the moment?
_____

6 Where is Antonio today?
_____

4 ⭐⭐⭐ Answer the questions with your own ideas.

1 Do you prefer playing sports or watching them on TV? Why?
_____

2 Do you ever watch sports live? Which ones?
_____

 Channel 1 Sports @Channel1Sports
It's the day of the UEFA Champions League Final, and you can see it live on our sports show from eight o'clock tonight or later, on demand, from 11! More than 4 billion people watch soccer on TV. Are you one of them? Tweet us and tell us: Are you watching or playing sports right now?

 Manny Ellis @MEllis
I want to watch basketball on TV today, but my sister's here with her friend. They're sitting in the living room and watching a really bad comedy show! So I'm in the kitchen watching the game on a tiny tablet!

 Amy Mount @aMount
I'm at my friend's house, and we're waiting for the big final to begin on Channel 1. We love watching sports on TV. We often play soccer too, but today we're eating snacks and supporting our team.

 Channel 1 Sports @Channel1Sports
Right now on Channel 1, we're showing a documentary about the history of the Olympics. Here's an interesting fact: Around 3.5 billion people watched the last Olympics! But what do you think – do more people watch the Olympics or the World Cup Final? Which other sports are good to watch on TV?

 Antonio González @toni2020
I think cycling's a great sport to watch on TV, but today I'm standing on the side of the road watching the competitors in my country's famous three-week event: the _Vuelta a España_! They're doing a very long part of the race today: over 200 km in one day!

GRAMMAR IN ACTION
Present Continuous

1 ⭐ (Circle) the correct options.

1 In my school, we *learning* / *('re learning)* how to edit videos.

2 Leni *is making* / *is makeing* clothes for the school production.

3 Helena and Jack *are watch* / *are watching* their favorite show.

4 Who *is sitting* / *is siting* next to you in class today?

5 My brother *isn't eating* / *not eating* much at the moment.

6 *Are you waiting* / *You waiting* for the news to begin?

2 ⭐ Complete the sentences with the present continuous form of the verbs in parentheses.

1 She *'s chatting* (chat) with her friends online.

2 He _____ (prepare) his history presentation.

3 We _____ (wait) for the school bus.

4 He _____ (make) a video about skateboarders.

5 They _____ (not cry); they _____ (laugh).

6 I _____ (not watch) anything; I _____ (work)!

3 ⭐⭐ Put the words in the correct order to make questions. Then match them with the answers from Exercise 2.

a those / crying / are / Why / boys / ?

  Why are those boys crying? ⑤

b on the computer / Anita / doing / What / is / ?

  _____ ☐

c you / there / all / Why / standing / are / ?

  _____ ☐

d park / doing / the / Miguel / What / is / at / ?

  _____ ☐

e Why / late / working / is / tonight / Paul / ?

  _____ ☐

f you / What / watching / are / on TV / ?

  _____ ☐

4 ⭐⭐ Write questions and short answers with the present continuous.

1 you / cycle / to school? (✓)

  Are you cycling to school? _____ *Yes, I am.*

2 we / listen / to the instructor? (✗)

  _____ _____

3 she / wait / for the next episode? (✓)

  _____ _____

4 they / enjoy / the show? (✗)

  _____ _____

5 you / send / a message to a friend? (✗)

  _____ _____

6 I / help / you? (✓)

  _____ _____

5 ⭐⭐ Complete the email with the correct present continuous form of the verbs in the box.

> learn   look forward to   ~~not use~~
> prepare   take   use   work   write

● ● ●

Dear Uncle Dominic,

Mom tells me you have a new camera and that you want to give me your old one because you ¹ *aren't using* it. Great! I hear it's better than the one I ² _____ at the moment, so I ³ _____ this email to say thank you! ⁴ _____ you _____ lots of great photos now with your new camera?

I ⁵ _____ a presentation for my media studies class with a classmate this week. We ⁶ _____ a lot about taking black and white photos – it's interesting! We ⁷ _____ on a series of winter photos. So I ⁸ _____ the new camera very much!

Thanks again and see you soon.

Jo

VOCABULARY AND LISTENING
Making Movies

1 ⭐ **Complete the crossword. Use the clues.**

Across

3 Please move those … . They're shining in my eyes.

5 I'm wearing a gorilla … , and I'm getting very hot!

8 A sound … knows when the actors are too quiet or too loud.

10 I'm hoping to be a camera … when I finish school.

Down

1 Marius is writing the … for his documentary project.

2 Where are they building the … for the new soap opera?

4 The best … in *The Hunger Games* is Josh Hutcherson.

6 A … artist named Lucy is making that young woman look older.

7 The … is just sitting in her chair and telling us what to do.

9 I can take great photos with my new digital … .

2 ⭐ **Match 1–5 with a–e.**

1 She's a top makeup artist,   [b]

2 You can take hundreds of photos ☐

3 The sound engineer ☐

4 Steven Spielberg ☐

5 The studio goes dark ☐

a is a famous movie director.

b and she can change actors' appearances.

c when the lights go out.

d is wearing big headphones.

e with a digital camera.

A Guided Tour

🎧 **3** ⭐⭐ **Listen to a girl on a tour of a soap opera set and answer the questions.**
1.01

1 In which city do they film the soap opera? _____

2 How many families are in the soap opera? _____

3 What is the street on the soap opera called? _____

🎧 **4** ⭐⭐ **Listen again and ⓒircle the correct answers.**
1.01

1 What is the name of the soap opera?

  a *Best Friends*   b *Teenlife*   ⓒ *Time of Our Lives*

2 One of the main actors is named … .

  a Adele Johnson   b Tom Bridges   c Lauren Thomas

3 The soap opera is about … .

  a teenagers' lives   b a mail carrier   c a school in Sydney

4 There are … houses on Clifton Street.

  a 15   b 20   c 100

5 There are … actors in the soap opera.

  a 10   b 50   c 60

5 ⭐⭐⭐ **Answer the questions.**

1 Which series do you like?

_____

2 What are the most popular soap operas in your country?

_____

GRAMMAR IN ACTION
Simple Present and Present Continuous

1 ⭐ **Complete the chart with the time expressions in the box.**

> ~~always~~   at the moment   every day
> every week   never   right now
> this afternoon   today

Simple Present	Present Continuous
always	

2 ⭐ **Complete the sentences with the simple present or present continuous form of the verbs in parentheses.**

1 She _'s waiting_ (wait) for her favorite TV show to start.
2 Actors _____ (love) taking selfies with their fans.
3 It usually _____ (take) days to learn the words of a script.
4 We _____ (watch) the news together at the moment.
5 I _____ (not come) here very often.
6 They _____ (make) a new episode every week.

3 ⭐⭐ **Put the words in the correct order to make sentences.**

1 download / Internet / Do / always / from / you / the / movies / ?

   Do you always download movies from the Internet?

2 drama / good / I'm / the / a / moment / TV / watching / at / .

   _____

3 outside / eat / sometimes / summer / We / lunch / our / the / in / .

   _____

4 talks / actors / to / sound engineer / the / The / never / .

   _____

5 you / listening / teacher / your / now / right / Are / to / ?

   _____

6 now / taking / Sydney / guided tour / a / My / is / sister / of / .

   _____

Adverbs of Manner

4 ⭐⭐ <u>Underline</u> and correct one mistake in each sentence.

1 My mother isn't a <u>slowly</u> driver. ____slow____
2 Their little brothers are playing happyly.

   _____

3 Our parents teach us to say "thank you" nice.

   _____

4 Be carefully! That camera is very expensive!

   _____

5 You're doing your homework very good at the moment. _____
6 She's playing the guitar beautiful now.

   _____

5 ⭐⭐ **Choose the correct adjectives. Then complete the sentences with the adverb forms.**

1 My brother writes very ____well____ (good / bad). I enjoy reading his stories.
2 Leila speaks very _____ (loud / quiet). I can't hear what she's saying sometimes.
3 That movie starts _____ (slow / fast). The beginning is really boring.
4 Kitty is singing really _____ (loud / quiet). You can hear her in the street!
5 You work _____ (easy / hard). That's why you do well on your tests.
6 This book ends _____ (good / bad). I don't like the ending at all.

WRITING
A Description of a Celebrity

1 ⭐ **Read the description. Why can you watch Mason Millerson videos with your parents?**

_____

My Favorite Comedian
By Gabriel Costa

1 Mason Millerson is my favorite comedian. He's an Australian comedian, Internet personality, singer, writer, and actor. His comedy videos have over 2 billion views, and he has over 15 million subscribers.

2 In each video, Mason is really funny and very original. You can watch his videos on the Internet. On them, he just speaks to the camera in a very natural way, and you're laughing all the time. Sometimes I laugh so much that I cry! He talks about ordinary, everyday things, like eating dinner with family or waiting for a train, but he makes them special.

3 I really like Mason Millerson because he has a great imagination. His stories are funny, but they are never mean or offensive; so it's OK to watch Mason's videos with your parents. I think he's great!

2 ⭐⭐ **Read the description again and answer the questions.**

1 Where is Mason from? _____

2 How many people watch Mason's videos online regularly? _____

3 What sometimes happens when Gabriel watches Mason's videos? _____

3 ⭐ **Match the start of each paragraph (a–c) with the topics (1–3).**

a In each video, Mason is … ⬜

b I really like Mason Millerson because … ⬜

c Mason Millerson is my favorite comedian. ⬜

1 an introduction to the person and his videos

2 what the person's videos are usually about

3 why I like this person

4 ⭐ **Complete the sentences from the description and match them with the rules (a–c).**

1 He's an Australian comedian, Internet personality, singer, writer, _____ actor. ⬜

2 He talks about ordinary, everyday things … , _____ he makes them special. ⬜

3 His stories are … never mean _____ offensive. ⬜

a We use _but_ to show different information.

b We use _or_ when there is a choice of two or more things.

c We use _and_ to add similar information.

PLAN

5 ⭐⭐ **Write a description of your favorite comedian or comedy actor. Take notes about these things.**

1 Who the person is: _____

What they do: _____

How many followers they have:

_____

2 What they usually do in their videos or movies:

_____

3 Why I like this person and their videos or movies:

_____

WRITE

6 ⭐⭐⭐ **Write your description. Remember to include three paragraphs using the information from Exercise 5, the correct present tenses, and adverbs, and _and_, _but_, and _or_.**

CHECK

7 **Do you …**

• use sentences with _and_, _but_, and _or_?

• give information about what the person usually does?

• explain why you like the person?

1 REVIEW

VOCABULARY

1 Match 1–8 with a–h.

1 I don't like cooking shows ☐
2 They're talking about the soccer match ☐
3 Disney is famous for ☐
4 Dad's watching a comedy, ☐
5 Ava's watching the documentary ☐
6 I love historical dramas about ☐
7 You can win a lot of money ☐
8 Do you usually watch the news ☐

a about animals in Africa.
b on some of these game shows.
c on TV or online?
d but he doesn't think it's funny.
e children's cartoons.
f on our favorite sports show.
g life in the 1500s.
h because I hate cooking.

2 Complete the sentences with the words in the box.

> actor   camera operator   costume   digital camera   director   lights
> makeup artist   script   set   sound engineer

1 The _____ is filming the pandas up close and getting some great shots.
2 Carlos learns the words by reading his _____ many times.
3 Does a TV news anchor wear normal clothes or a _____ ?
4 The movie _____ tells everyone what to do and how to do it.
5 It can be very hot when you work under bright studio _____ .
6 The _____ for my favorite series is a street in Mexico City.
7 A _____ changes people's appearances for movies.
8 The _____ knows when the actors are speaking very quietly.
9 The _____ who plays the son is only six years old.
10 I can make great home videos with my new _____ .

GRAMMAR IN ACTION

3 Complete the conversation with the present continuous form of the verbs in parentheses.

PEDRO What ¹_____ (you / do)?

MARIA I ²_____ (write) an email to my uncle. He ³_____ (work) on a movie set at the moment.

PEDRO Wow! ⁴_____ (he / film) any famous actors?

MARIA No, he isn't. He ⁵_____ (travel) with the film crew and actors, and he ⁶_____ (cook) their food. He's a chef.

PEDRO That's cool. So why ⁷_____ (you / send) him an email?

MARIA I ⁸_____ (hope) he can come to my birthday party and cook something good for me!

4 Complete the sentences with the simple present or present continuous form of the verbs in parentheses.

1 I _____ (write) to my friend in Los Angeles right now. I _____ (email) her every month.

2 We usually _____ (watch) the news on TV, but today we _____ (listen) to it in the car.

3 Henry _____ (save) money at the moment because he _____ (need) a new bike.

4 _____ you _____ (look) for my sister? She usually _____ (sit) over there.

5 Our mom _____ (not go) to work on Fridays, but she _____ (work) today.

6 My friends _____ (swim) at the beach today, but I'm not. I _____ (prefer) swimming pools.

7 _____ you _____ (wait) for Susie? She _____ usually _____ (not arrive) late.

8 I _____ (cook) pancakes for breakfast at the moment. I often _____ (make) them on the weekend.

5 (Circle) the correct options.

1 Please be *quiet* / *quietly*! Your baby sister is sleeping.

2 Sandra is a very *nice* / *nicely* girl, in my opinion.

3 The children are watching *Frozen 2* and eating ice cream *happy* / *happily*.

4 I always speak *loud* / *loudly*, but Grandpa still can't hear me.

5 When we work *quick* / *quickly*, we sometimes make mistakes.

6 He answered the questions *good* / *well* on the test.

7 Our music teacher plays the guitar *beautiful* / *beautifully*.

8 Catalina is wearing a very *pretty* / *prettily* costume in the show.

6 Complete the conversation with the missing words. (Circle) the correct options.

ANA Hi, Dan. [1]_____ your vacation?

DAN We [2]_____ a great time here. I [3]_____ with my friends and their family in their summer apartment.

ANA That's [4]_____. What do you think of it?

DAN It's [5]_____ and there's a pool.

ANA Lucky you! [6]_____ swimming every day?

DAN Well, my friends Tess and Rob [7]_____ every morning before breakfast.

ANA Great!

DAN Yeah, but actually I [8]_____ eating something first.

ANA Really?

DAN I'm always [9]_____ when I [10]_____ up!

ANA So when do you [11]_____ breakfast?

DAN Well, that's breakfast time for me – when I [12]_____ up.

		a	b	c
1	a	Enjoy you	b Are you enjoying	c You enjoy
2	a	have	b has	c 're having
3	a	'm staying	b stay	c staying
4	a	nice	b nicily	c nicely
5	a	beautifully	b beautiful	c beautifuly
6	a	Are you go	b Go you	c Do you go
7	a	swims	b are swiming	c swim
8	a	prefer	b 'm preferring	c 'm prefer
9	a	hungrily	b hungry	c hungryly
10	a	'm waking	b wakes	c wake
11	a	usually eat	b eat usually	c usual eat
12	a	'm getting	b gets	c get

How was the past different?

VOCABULARY
The Weather

1 ⭐ **Find 12 more weather words in the word snake.**

snowyfoggycoldwindyhoticycloudyrainywarmsunnywetstormydry

2 ⭐ **Circle the correct options.**

1 We have winter coats because it is a *cold* / *warm* day.

2 Be careful, don't run! It's *hot* / *icy* outside.

3 It's not much fun skiing when it's *rainy* / *snowy*.

4 The bus driver can't see the road. It's very *windy* / *foggy* today.

5 **A** Is it raining now? **B** No, but it's *wet* / *cloudy*.

6 Trees sometimes fall down in very *windy* / *warm* weather.

3 ⭐⭐ **Complete the sentences with the words in the box. Then match them with photos a–f.**

foggy snowy ~~stormy~~ sunny wet windy

1 It's dangerous to go surfing in ___stormy___ weather. ☐f

2 We can't have a picnic today. The grass is very _____ because of the rain. ☐

3 It's _____, and they are lost because they can't see. ☐

4 On a _____ day, they wear their hats, gloves, and scarves. ☐

5 This _____ weather is perfect for sailing. ☐

6 It's _____, so don't forget your sunglasses! ☐

4 ⭐⭐ **Complete the email with words from Exercise 1.**

TO: Jeremy

FROM: Calum

Dear Jeremy,

What's the weather like where you are? Here it's beautiful and ¹___sunny___, and I'm sitting under a tree with a sun hat and sunglasses on. There's no rain, so the fields are very ²_____. I like ³_____ weather – about 20 °C is fine, but 35 °C is very ⁴_____ and not great for me! We usually get a lot of ⁵_____ days in Oregon, so it's often very wet, but not this year. Actually, I can't wait for the winter, with some nice ⁶_____ weekends for skiing.

Talk to you soon,
Calum

5 ⭐⭐ **Write the noun forms of the adjectives.**

1 rainy _____rain_____

2 cloudy _____

3 icy _____

4 sunny _____

5 windy _____

6 snowy _____

7 foggy _____

8 stormy _____

Explore It! 🖱

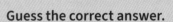

Guess the correct answer.

The Sami people live in the far north of Norway, Sweden, Finland, and Russia. Language experts say that the Sami have at least *8 / 18 / 180* words for snow and ice.

Find another interesting fact about the Sami people. Write a question and send it to a classmate in an email, or ask them in the next class.

READING
Diary Extracts

1 ⭐ **Read the text and diary extracts. What did Ollie and Jack find on their journey?**

_____

Looking for Treasure

In 2010, an American man hid a big box full of treasure somewhere in the Rocky Mountains. His name is Forrest Fenn, and he was over 80 years old at the time. Fenn is an art expert, and he had a lot of old and very expensive objects. He filled his box with jewelry, diamonds, and gold, and then buried it in a secret place in the mountains. Why did he do that? He wanted to give families a reason to enjoy time in nature. In his opinion, children spend a lot of time on computers and need to do more outdoor activities. The result? Thousands of people are looking for Forrest Fenn's treasure. Below are diary extracts from two young treasure hunters.

Ollie's Diary: May 2, 2020

My friend Jack and I are on vacation in Yellowstone National Park, and we're looking for buried treasure with our parents. They planned this trip because they wanted us to enjoy hiking and camping in the spring. I just want to find the box! Forrest Fenn wrote a 24-line poem with clues about where to find it. He shared the poem on Instagram, so we know the box is somewhere in Wyoming or Colorado – two of the BIGGEST STATES in the U.S.A.!

Jack's Diary: May 11, 2020

Time to go home, but the roads are closed and there's deep snow everywhere. We're all staying in a hostel because it's not possible to camp out in this weather. It's very cold and there's no Wi-Fi here. And the worst thing is that we didn't find any treasure! I don't think this was a good idea after all!

2 ⭐⭐ **Read the text and diary extracts again and check the meaning of these words in a dictionary. Then complete the sentences.**

> bury   clues   hides   ~~jewelry~~
> secret   treasure

1 That ___jewelry___ store sells beautiful earrings, necklaces, and bracelets.
2 That dog is making a hole in the ground to _____ the ball!
3 She usually _____ her diary under her bed.
4 Grandma keeps her diamond ring in a _____ place in her house.
5 They found a ship on the ocean floor with lots of _____ in it.
6 I always read the _____ carefully when I'm doing a crossword.

3 ⭐⭐ **Read the text again. Are the sentences _T_ (true) or _F_ (false)?**

1 Forrest Fenn hid expensive jewelry and gold in a box.   T
2 He hid the box because he doesn't want people to find it.   ___
3 The boys' parents didn't go with them.   ___
4 Fenn's clues are on the Internet.   ___
5 The boys can't get home because of the weather.   ___
6 Jack enjoyed hunting for treasure.   ___

4 ⭐⭐⭐ **Answer the questions with your own ideas.**

1 What outdoor activities do you do?

_____

2 Do you like the idea of this treasure hunt? Why / Why not?

_____

GRAMMAR IN ACTION
Simple Past

1 ☆ **Complete the sentences with the simple past form of the verbs in parentheses.**

1 The boys ____hiked____ (hike) for nine days.
2 They _____ (take) Fenn's clues with them.
3 They _____ (enjoy) listening to the poem about the buried treasure.
4 The adults and children _____ (read) the clues carefully.
5 Some people _____ (write) diaries about their journey.
6 Actually, the diary extracts _____ (be) very interesting.

2 ☆☆ **Complete the questions with the words in the box. Then match the questions with the answers from Exercise 1.**

> did (x2)   enjoy   hike   were   write

a What ____did____ the adults and children read carefully? [4]
b How long did the boys _____ for? ☐
c _____ the diary extracts boring? ☐
d What did they _____ listening to? ☐
e What _____ they take with them? ☐
f What did some people _____? ☐

3 ☆☆ **Write questions and short answers in the simple past.**

1 you / have a good vacation, Tina? (✓)
  Did you have a good vacation, Tina?   _Yes, I did._
2 you / swim in the ocean? (✗)
  _____   _____
3 you all / go in the pool? (✓)
  _____   _____
4 your friends / like the food? (✓)
  _____   _____
5 Tomas / take lots of photos? (✓)
  _____   _____
6 Susie / want to come home? (✗)
  _____   _____

4 ☆☆ **Underline and correct one mistake in each sentence.**

1 Henry <u>seed</u> photos of the pioneers yesterday.
  ____saw____
2 We didn't enjoyed the bus trip. _____
3 Did you found a good tour guide last week?
  _____
4 I did went out in the stormy weather. _____
5 They stoped for food and drink. _____
6 Did she be late for class yesterday? _____

5 ☆☆ **Complete the conversation with the correct simple past form of the verbs in the box.**

> become   decide   not have   return
> ride   s̶e̶e̶   stay   take care of   travel   write

IVAN   [1] ____Did____ you ____see____ the TV documentary about Dervla Murphy last night?

DARIA   No, I didn't. Who is she?

IVAN   An amazing traveler and travel writer. In 1963, she [2]_____ to cycle from her hometown in Ireland all the way to India. And in those days, people [3]_____ the kinds of bikes we have now!

DARIA   [4]_____ she _____ her bike all the way to India?

IVAN   Yes, she did, and she [5]_____ there for a year. She [6]_____ Tibetan refugee children there, and when she [7]_____ home, she [8]_____ her first book. She quickly [9]_____ a famous travel writer – there are more than 20 books by her. Dervla [10]_____ all over the world when she was younger, but she still can't drive a car!

VOCABULARY AND LISTENING
Useful Objects

A Radio Show

1 ⭐ **Put the letters in the correct order to make words for useful objects.**

1 r r r o i m   _mirror_
2 m p l a
3 l k t e b n a
4 o n o p s
5 i n f e k
6 w p l o l i
7 w b l o
8 k r o f
9 b c m o
10 l e t p a
11 s s s s o c i r
12 u p c
13 b h i r a u s h r
14 h t b t u h o s o r

2 ⭐⭐ **Match the photos with six words from Exercise 1.**

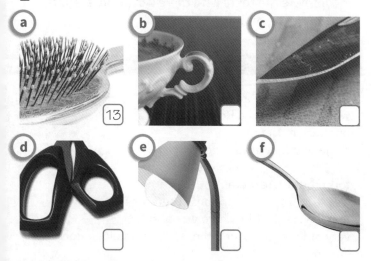

a   `13`
b
c
d
e
f

3 ⭐ **Where do you usually find the objects from Exercise 1? Some words can go in more than one category.**

Kitchen	Bathroom	Bedroom
knife		

🎧 **4** ⭐ **Listen to a radio show about a volcanic eruption. Mark (✓) the words you hear.**
2.01

comb ✓   fork ☐   jewelry ☐
lamp ☐   mirror ☐   museum ☐
school ☐   scissors ☐

🎧 **5** ⭐⭐ **Listen again and complete the sentences.**
2.01

1 Sam works at a ___history museum___ in London.
2 The volcano destroyed two cities in _____ hours.
3 In the _____, archaeologists found a lot of everyday objects buried in the cities.
4 In one of the cities, they found a baby's _____.
5 One man died when a rock hit him on the _____.
6 Under his body, they found a bag with money and a _____.

6 ⭐⭐⭐ **Complete the sentences so they are true for you.**

1 *I'd like / I wouldn't like* to visit Pompeii and Herculaneum because _____ .

2 *I'd like / I wouldn't like* to visit Sam's display in London because _____ .

GRAMMAR IN ACTION
There Was/Were

1 ⭐ Circle the correct options.

1 (There was) / *There were* a team of archaeologists in Naples.

2 *There was* / *There were* some kitchen furniture in the exhibition.

3 *Was there* / *Were there* any travelers in the storm?

4 *There wasn't* / *There weren't* any information about the objects.

5 *Was there* / *Were there* a school in Herculaneum?

6 *There was* / *There were* some old books in the box.

7 *There wasn't* / *There weren't* any clothes in the ruins.

2 ⭐⭐ Put the words in the correct order to make sentences.

1 wasn't / rain / month / There / any / last / .

<u>There wasn't any rain last month.</u>

2 display / any / There / the / weren't / interesting / in / things / .

_____

3 people / exhibition / there / the / at / many / Were / ?

_____

4 old / baby / with / an / woman / There / a / was / .

_____

5 there / box / Was / any / the / jewelry / in / ?

_____

6 Naples / hundreds / were / in / tourists / There / of / .

_____

3 ⭐ Match 1–6 with a–f.

1 There were some [e]

2 Was there a ☐

3 There weren't any ☐

4 There was an ☐

5 Was there any ☐

6 Were there any ☐

a interesting display of jewelry.

b information about Herculaneum?

c useful objects in the kitchen?

d women on the team.

e Roman bowls in the museum.

f mirror in the woman's bag?

4 ⭐⭐ Complete the email with *some, any, a,* or *an.*

● ● ●

TO: Lily

FROM: Tom

Hi, Lily!

How are you? Just a quick email to tell you about our trip to Brazil! Yesterday, there was [1] <u>a</u> big storm, so we had a day of culture. We walked around the city, and there was [2] _____ fascinating museum called the Museum of Tomorrow, so we decided to go in. It's [3] _____ science museum in Rio, but [4] _____ architect from Spain designed it. There were [5] _____ amazing exhibitions about our planet, and there was [6] _____ very interesting information about it, too. There weren't [7] _____ postcards in the museum gift shop, but there was [8] _____ interesting little book, so I bought you that! Hope you like it!

Talk to you soon,
Tom

5 ⭐⭐ Look at the two museum displays and complete the texts with *there was(n't)/were(n't), a, an, some,* or *any.*

| Home | News | **Blog** | Lifestyle | |

[1] <u>There was</u> an interesting display with objects from a Roman kitchen at our local museum. [2] _____ some wooden bowls and [3] _____ knives and forks, but there weren't [4] _____ spoons. There was [5] _____ metal water bottle. There was also [6] _____ very old bread – over a thousand years old, in fact. Yummy!

My favorite display had beautiful objects from a woman's bedroom. There was [7] _____ old mirror and [8] _____ gold jewelry. She was probably [9] _____ important person. [10] _____ a beautiful necklace and a bracelet, too, but [11] _____ any earrings. And there was a comb with [12] _____ human hair in it!

WRITING
A Fictional Account of a Journey

1 ⭐ **Read the account and** (circle) **the best title.**

   a Swedish Family Lost in Edale

   b Help for Teenage Hikers in Sweden

   c Safe Return of Lost Hikers

● ● ●

Three Swedish teenagers decided to do a famous long-distance hike from England to Scotland. ¹ *They set off on* October 22, 2018, from Edale, a small village in northern England.

The walk is 412 km long, and Lucas, Sven, and Lilly wanted to complete it in three weeks. They wore big boots and carried heavy bags with their camping equipment. ²_____ it was warm and sunny, but after two days, everything changed. ³_____ cold and rainy. The hikers' boots got wet, and their bags got heavier.

The three friends didn't stop, but ⁴_____ _____ with the weather. On day four, it became foggy.
The path was difficult to see and they got lost. Then Sven fell and broke his leg. There was no one to help them and no cell phone signal.

⁵_____ on October 27, a mountain rescue team found the friends, and they arrived home safely the next day. Now they are planning to do the hike again in the spring.

2 ⭐⭐ **Complete the account with the words and phrases in the box.**

> At first,   Finally,   The weather was
> there were a lot of problems   ~~They set off on~~

3 ⭐ (Circle) **the correct options.**

   1 The teenagers wanted to hike from *Scotland to England* / *England to Scotland*.

   2 They hoped to do the hike in three *weeks* / *days*.

   3 The weather was *good* / *bad* on the first two days.

   4 *Lucas* / *Sven* had an accident.

4 ⭐ **Match 1–6 with a–f.**

1	October 22, 2018	`b`	**a** the day they arrived home
2	412 km	☐	**b** the day they set off
3	after two days	☐	**c** Lucas, Sven, and Lilly
4	the three friends	☐	**d** the length of the trip
5	October 28, 2018	☐	**e** when the friends plan to start again
6	in the spring	☐	**f** the weather changed

PLAN

5 ⭐⭐ **Write a fictional account of a journey. Make notes for each paragraph.**

   1 Who made the journey: _____

      _____

      When and where it started: _____

      _____

      Where they planned to go: _____

      _____

   2 The first part of the journey: _____

      _____

      The weather: _____

   3 How the journey continued: _____

      _____

      Any problems: _____

      _____

   4 The end of the journey: _____

WRITE

6 ⭐⭐⭐ **Write your fictional account. Remember to include the simple past, *there was/were*, and phrases from the *Useful Language* box (see Student's Book, p29).**

CHECK

7 **Do you …**

   • use the simple past to talk about the past?

   • put the events in the correct order?

   • explain what the journey was like?

VOCABULARY

1 Complete the sentences with weather words. Use the first letter to help you.

1 When it's f_____, it's difficult to see where you're going.

2 It's going to be r_____, so don't forget your umbrella.

3 She wore a hoodie, a scarf, and gloves because it was very c_____.

4 Don't run outside. It's i_____ and you can easily fall.

5 The weather was nice and w_____. We could swim every day.

6 A branch of the old tree broke on a very s_____ night.

7 It's still c_____, but it isn't raining anymore.

8 They could eat in the backyard because the weather was d_____.

9 The sun was really h_____, so Sally went inside.

10 I love winter evenings when it's s_____ outside.

11 On one horrible w_____ and w_____ night, the rain blew into our tent.

12 Take your sunglasses because it's very s_____ today.

2 Match the descriptions with the words in the box.

> blanket bowl comb cup fork hairbrush
> lamp mirror pillow plate scissors
> spoon toothbrush

1 You can use these to cut hair or paper. _____

2 This helps you to see when it's dark. _____

3 Two objects you use for your hair. _____ _____

4 You need this to clean your teeth. _____

5 Two useful objects you use to put food in your mouth.

_____ _____

6 You use this at night to keep warm. _____

7 You put soup in a _____ and a sandwich on a _____.

8 You put your tea or coffee in this. _____

9 Your head is on this when you're sleeping in bed.

_____

10 You look into this when you're combing your hair.

_____

GRAMMAR IN ACTION

3 Choose the correct verbs. Then write the simple past form of the verb.

Vasco da Gama, a Portuguese sailor and explorer, [1](work / arrive) _____ on the king's ships from 1492. In July 1497, he [2](leave / set) _____ off on a journey to India. He [3](want / become) _____ to find a route to the Far East. He [4](take / travel) _____ a total of 38,600 km. The journey [5](be / go) _____ dangerous, and the weather [6](like / be) _____ often stormy. Da Gama [7](take / carry) _____ 170 men with him, but only 54 [8](arrive / stay) _____ home safely in 1499.

4 Complete the sentences with the correct form of *there was/were* and *a, an, some,* or *any*.

1 _____ mirrors in the bathroom. (–)

2 _____ information about Egyptian mummies?

3 _____ interesting books in the museum gift shop. (+)

4 _____ article about dinosaurs in the newspaper. (+)

5 _____ good exhibitions in Berlin?

6 _____ clear answer to my question. (–)

7 _____ bowls in the kitchen. (–)

8 _____ visitors from Portugal in our school. (+)

CUMULATIVE GRAMMAR

5 Complete the conversation with the missing words. (Circle) the correct options.

SARA   Hi, Katie. What ¹_____ at the moment?

KATIE   I'm working really ²_____ ! I need some ideas for my history project.

SARA   ³_____ the documentary about English kings and queens last Saturday?

KATIE   No, I ⁴_____ camping last weekend, so I missed it.

SARA   That's a shame. It was very ⁵_____ .

KATIE   ⁶_____ information about the clothes they wore in the past?

SARA   Yes, and ⁷_____ interesting facts about jewelry. I ⁸_____ about how they made gold and silver artifacts for my history project.

KATIE   I know! I can write about everyday objects in the 16th century.

SARA   ⁹_____ exhibition in the city library last month called "At Home in the Past."

KATIE   Really?

SARA   And ¹⁰_____ presentation by a famous history professor.

KATIE   Oh, wow. I ¹¹_____ that, too. I really am a terrible student!

SARA   Don't worry. I ¹²_____ to that presentation, so I can help you.

KATIE   Really? You're a great friend. Thanks, Sara!

1	a do you	b did you do	c are you doing
2	a hardly	b hard	c harder
3	a Saw you	b Did you saw	c Did you see
4	a went	b go	c didn't go
5	a well	b good	c better
6	a Was there any	b Were there any	c Was there an
7	a was there some	b weren't there any	c there were some
8	a write	b 'm writting	c 'm writing
9	a There's an	b There was an	c There was a
10	a there was a	b was there a	c there was an
11	a was missing	b misses	c missed
12	a go	b went	c going

3 What do stories teach us?

VOCABULARY
Adjectives of Feeling

1 ⭐ **Read the clues and complete the puzzle. Then complete sentence 11 with your own idea.**

Crossword:
1 (across) L O N E L Y
11 (down) E M B A R R A S S E D

1 I feel … when I have nobody to talk to.
2 When you have nothing to do, you get … .
3 I don't like big spiders, and I feel … when I see one.
4 Before an important test or exam, you can feel … .
5 My parents sometimes get … when I arrive home late.
6 Do your teachers get … when you don't listen to them?
7 I was … to see my friend because she arrived a day early!
8 They were very … when they heard your sad news.
9 Young children get … about their birthdays.
10 You look … . Why don't you go to bed?
11 I feel embarrassed when _____
_____ .

2 ⭐ **Circle the correct options.**

1 Leave the light on when you feel **afraid** / angry of the dark.
2 Was your brother *excited* / *angry* when you took his tablet?
3 Call a friend when you feel *tired* / *lonely* and want some company.
4 I'm never *excited* / *bored*; there's always something to do.
5 Julio was *embarrassed* / *lonely* because he didn't remember my name.

3 ⭐⭐ **Complete the email with the words in the box.**

> excited   nervous   ~~surprised~~   tired   upset

● ● ●

TO: Diana   FROM: Kylie

Dear Diana,

Hi! How are you? I was
¹ _surprised_ when you weren't
in class today. Are you
² _____ about the
exam tomorrow? I can't study anymore tonight. I'm very
³ _____ – I need to go to bed. My parents
get ⁴ _____ when I work late – they think
I need more sleep! Don't worry about tomorrow. Just
remember our camping trip when the exams are
over – I'm ⁵ _____ about that!

See you, Kylie

4 ⭐⭐⭐ **Complete the sentences so they are true for you. Write them in your notebook.**

I feel nervous when … .   I don't get upset when … .
I sometimes feel lonely when … .

Explore It!

Guess the correct answer.

If you have hippophilia, you love *hippos* / *spiders* / *horses* and they make you feel good.

Find another interesting thing that makes people feel good. Write a question and send it to a classmate in an email, or ask them in the next class.

READING
A Folk Tale

1 ⭐ **Read the folk tale and match the names (1–3) with the people (a–c).**

1 Manata ☐   a the young man
2 Matakauri ☐   b the terrible giant
3 Matau ☐   c the beautiful girl

The Story of Lake Wakatipu

The Māori people of New Zealand have different stories about their country and how it began. One popular Māori story is about Lake Wakatipu. This lake is in the shape of the letter *S*, and there are high mountains all around it.

The story is about the beautiful daughter of a Māori chief. Her name was Manata, and she loved a young man named Matakauri. They wanted to get married, but Manata's father said no because Matakauri was not important. One day, a terrible giant named Matau came down from the mountains and took Manata. Her father was very upset and worried. "The man who rescues Manata can ask her to marry him," he said. Many men were afraid of the giant because he was very strong and dangerous. But Matakauri's love for Manata was strong, too, so he rescued her and she became his wife.

However, Matakauri was unhappy because the giant was still alive. One winter day, he went back to the giant's home. Matau was sleeping on a bed of dry leaves when Matakauri started a fire under him. Soon Matau's body was burning, although his heart was still beating. The giant's dead body made a big hole in the ground, in the shape of the letter *S*. The snow on the mountains melted because of the fire and ran into the hole. This created Lake Wakatipu.

Today, people still tell this story. The water in the lake goes up and down, and people say it is the beating heart of the dead giant!

2 ⭐⭐ **Read the folk tale again and check the meaning of the words in the box in a dictionary. Then complete the sentences.**

> beat   ~~burn~~   chief
> giant   melts   rescue

1 Cook the vegetables on low heat. Don't _____burn_____ them!
2 The _____ was the most important person in the village.
3 Ice cream _____ in the hot sun.
4 Heroes _____ people from dangerous situations.
5 Does your heart _____ faster when you're excited or nervous?
6 The _____ in the folk tale was ten meters tall!

3 ⭐⭐ **Are the sentences *T* (true) or *F* (false)?**

1 Manata's father wasn't an important person.   F
2 Matakauri was a chief.   ___
3 Matakauri and Manata got married after the giant died.   ___
4 Matau died in the water when the snow melted.   ___
5 Matau's body made a big hole that looked like a letter.   ___
6 People tell the story to explain why the water in Lake Wakatipu moves.   ___

4 ⭐⭐⭐ **Choose from the options and complete the sentences in your notebook so they are true for you.**

1 I *think / don't think* Matakauri was an important person because … .
2 I *like / don't like* the ending of this story because … .
3 I *believe / don't believe* folk tales are just for young children because … .

GRAMMAR IN ACTION
Past Continuous: Affirmative and Negative

1 ⭐ **Complete the sentences with the past continuous form of the verbs in parentheses.**

1 I _was working_ (work) all afternoon yesterday.

2 Yolanda _____ (make) sandwiches for our picnic.

3 My brother _____ (not sleep) in front of the TV.

4 We _____ (sit) in the car.

5 Clara _____ (look) for her phone.

6 They _____ (not shop) at the supermarket.

2 ⭐⭐ **Look at the photos and correct the sentences. Use the past continuous.**

1 She was playing soccer.

She wasn't playing soccer. She was playing tennis.

2 They were texting.

_____

_____

3 He was sleeping.

_____

_____

4 We were sitting on the bus.

_____

_____

3 ⭐⭐ **Complete the email with the past continuous form of the verbs in the box.**

feel   ~~have~~   jump   listen   not dance   play   sleep

● ● ●

Dear Irina,

Happy New Year! I hope you [1] _were having_ fun at midnight last night. I was at a party, and a DJ [2] _____ my favorite songs. I [3] _____ to the music, but I [4] _____ – I [5] _____ really tired. 😞 My friends [6] _____ up and down on the dance floor all night, though! What about you? Don't tell me that you [7] _____! 🙂

Write back soon!

Jessie

4 ⭐⭐⭐ **Look at the picture and complete the story with appropriate verbs in the past continuous. There may be more than one possibility.**

I had an interesting dream last night. I [1] _was sitting_ outside. It was winter. Everything was white because it [2] _____, and I was very cold because I [3] _____ winter clothes. A big brown bear [4] _____

in front of me on two legs. It was very tall! It looked angry and dangerous.
I don't know why, but I [5] _____ afraid at all. I [6] _____ nicely to the bear in a very friendly voice, but the bear [7] _____ to me! Then suddenly the bear [8] _____ a guitar and singing! In the end, I started to get angry with the bear. Then I woke up!

VOCABULARY AND LISTENING
Prepositions of Movement

1 ⭐ **Complete the prepositions with the missing vowels.**

1 u n d e r
2 _ p
3 _ c r _ s s
4 p _ s t
5 _ _ t _ f
6 t h r _ _ g h
7 _ n t _
8 b _ t w _ _ n
9 d _ w n
10 _ l _ n g
11 _ v _ r
12 _ f f

2 ⭐⭐ **Complete the sentences with the prepositions in the box.**

> ~~along~~ into off over through under

1 I was walking ____along____ the river yesterday afternoon.
2 They were having a picnic _____ the trees.
3 Our dog was running after a cat, but it jumped _____ a wall.
4 When she lost her keys, she climbed into her house _____ the open window.
5 We can get _____ the bus here and walk to my house.
6 Mom walked _____ the store and asked the assistant for help.

3 ⭐⭐ **Look at the photos and complete the sentences with prepositions from Exercise 1.**

1 He was running ____down____ the stairs.
2 Shelia was getting _____ the taxi.
3 The sisters were walking _____ their parents.
4 Jodie was going _____ the table.
5 Dominic was jumping _____ the water.
6 Dan was walking _____ the street.

A Radio Phone-in

4 ⭐ **Look at the picture. What do you think the story is about? Predict the words you might hear.**

_____

🎧 5 ⭐ **Listen to Bruno's story. Do you hear any of your words from Exercise 4?**
3.01

🎧 6 ⭐⭐ **Listen again and (circle) the correct answers.**
3.01

1 The radio show is about … things that happen to people.
a dangerous　　c embarrassing
ⓑ funny
2 When Bruno got off the bus, a man was running … .
a across the street　c out of a bank
b into a bank
3 The man had a … .
a knife in a bag　b knife　c bag
4 The alarm bells were ringing … .
a in the bus　　c outside the bank
b inside the bank
5 The people at the bus stop were … .
a helping the man
b not doing anything
c helping the police officer
6 The police officer caught the man because … stopped him.
a a woman　b Bruno　c some dogs

7 ⭐⭐⭐ **Answer the questions.**

1 How do you think the people at the bus stop felt?

_____

2 Did they do the right thing? Why / Why not?

_____

GRAMMAR IN ACTION
Past Continuous: Questions

1 ⭐ **Put the words in the correct order to make past continuous questions.**

1 you / watching / night / Were / last / news / the / ?

   Were you watching the news last night?

2 the / long / a / wearing / woman / coat / Was / ?

   _____

3 down / Were / street / your / skating / friends / the / ?

   _____

4 through / people / many / park / were / How / the / walking / ?

   _____

5 into / Where / children / river / were / the / the / jumping / ?

   _____

6 off / bus / the / passengers / were / Why / the / getting / ?

   _____

2 ⭐⭐ **Write past continuous questions and short answers about the story from Exercise 5 on page 27.**

1 A the man / wear / a hoodie / ?

   Was the man wearing a hoodie?

   B No, he wasn't.

2 A he / carry / a black bag / ?

   _____

   B _____

3 A alarm bells / ring / in the bank / ?

   _____

   B _____

4 A the police officer / ride / a motorcycle / ?

   _____

   B _____

5 A the people / help / the police officer / ?

   _____

   B _____

6 A the dogs / run after / the man / ?

   _____

   B _____

Simple Past and Past Continuous

3 ⭐⭐ Ⓒircle the correct options.

1 Our neighbor ⟨fell⟩ / was falling while he walked / ⟨was walking⟩ into the town.

2 While she looked / was looking for her bag, she found / was finding an old photo.

3 William didn't hear / wasn't hearing the man when he stood / was standing behind him.

4 We cycled / were cycling home when it started / was starting to rain.

5 She had / was having a problem when she did / was doing her homework.

6 Did they sit / Were they sitting on the bus when it hit / was hitting the car?

4 ⭐⭐ <u>Underline</u> **and correct one mistake in each sentence.**

1 Ann <u>did</u> her homework when her mother came into her room. ___*was doing*___

2 My friend was looking at her phone when the teacher was seeing her. _____

3 While we were eating dinner, the cat was jumping onto the table and surprised us! _____

4 He was playing football when he was breaking his leg. _____

5 Weren't you answering the phone when it rang?

   _____

5 ⭐⭐ **Complete the text with the correct past continuous or simple past form of the verbs in the box.**

leave	not look	not see	play
stand	steal	take	~~wait~~	walk

Caught on Camera!

I ¹ _was waiting_ for a friend at the park. I ² _____ under a small tree – that's why the girl ³ _____ me. She ⁴ _____ through the park quickly to where a man ⁵ _____ soccer with his son. The man's backpack was under a chair, and the girl ⁶ _____ it when he ⁷ _____ in her direction. While the girl ⁸ _____ the park, I ⁹ _____ a photo of her.

WRITING
A Story

1 ⭐ **Look at the notes. What do you think Olive's story is about? Read the story and check your ideas.**

A Misunderstanding
By Olive Crooke

The other day, I was playing tennis with some friends after school, and I got home late in the afternoon. At first, I thought my parents were working, but then I noticed the car wasn't outside. There was no one in the house. Then I remembered they were all shopping.

I went to get a snack, and I saw a note on the fridge from my dad. It said, "We were waiting for you, but it got late. Your dinner's in the fridge. Back soon." I found a bowl of food and took it out. It didn't look very good, but I was hungry, so I started to eat it. Suddenly, I saw another note on the table from my mom. It said, "Please feed the cat – her food's in a bowl in the fridge." I was eating the cat's dinner!

I didn't feel well, so the next morning I didn't go to school. The next day, I told my my brothers what happened. They thought it was very funny, but I wasn't laughing!

2 ⭐⭐ **Read the story again. Are the sentences *T* (true) or *F* (false)?**

1 Olive's story happened yesterday. ___F___

2 Her parents were at work. _____

3 Olive's parents expected her to arrive sooner. _____

4 She stayed at home the day after eating the cat food. _____

5 She thought it was a funny accident. _____

3 ⭐⭐ **Read the story again and put the events (a–g) in the correct order (1–7).**

a She didn't go to school the next day. ☐

b Olive was playing tennis. ☐1

c She found a note about her dinner. ☐

d She saw a note about the cat's dinner. ☐

e She found a bowl of food and started eating it. ☐

f She came home late and the house was empty. ☐

g She realized her mistake and felt sick. ☐

4 ⭐⭐ **Put the phrases in the order they appear in the story.**

a in the afternoon ☐   d At first, ☐

b The next day, ☐   e the next morning ☐

c Suddenly, ☐   f The other day, ☐1

PLAN
5 ⭐⭐ **Write a story. Think about a misunderstanding that happened to you, or invent one. Make notes about these things.**

1 What was happening before the main events started: _____

What happened first: _____

2 The main events of the story: _____

3 What happened in the end: _____

WRITE
6 ⭐⭐⭐ **Write your story. Remember to include three paragraphs using the information from Exercise 5, the simple past and past continuous, and phrases from the *Useful Language* box (see Student's Book, p41).**

CHECK
7 **Do you …**
- have three paragraphs?
- explain the main events?
- explain what happened in the end?

VOCABULARY

1 Complete the sentences with adjectives of feeling. Use the first letter to help you.

1 I'm w_____ about my sister because she isn't feeling very happy.

2 He felt e_____ when he didn't understand the message.

3 Linda is busy all the time! She's never b_____.

4 Don't be n_____ about your exams. You'll be fine.

5 Are you a_____ of cows? They're big, and they can get angry!

6 We were s_____ when some old friends from Mexico suddenly came to our door!

7 Sara felt l_____ at first when she moved to a new town. She didn't have any friends there.

8 Do your parents get a_____ when you come home late?

9 Don't get so e_____! It's only a little birthday present!

10 They were all t_____ after running and doing exercise all day.

11 Don't be u_____ when you don't get 100% on a test. No one gets that!

2 Match 1–6 with a–f.

1 They ran quickly down ☐

2 She was sitting between ☐

3 When you walk past ☐

4 We jumped off the boat ☐

5 Tell the driver your address ☐

6 Look right, left, and then right again ☐

a when you get into the taxi.

b into the river.

c her two best friends.

d before you walk across the street.

e my house, you can always come in.

f the stairs and out into the street.

3 Look at the photos and circle the correct prepositions.

1 The boat went *across / under* the bridge.

2 Kim was running *down / across* the road.

3 He jumped *through / over* the wall.

4 The cat came *through / under* the kitchen window.

5 The movie star got *out of / off of* the car.

6 Lena climbed *over / up* a tree.

GRAMMAR IN ACTION

4 Complete the email with the past continuous form of the verbs in the box.

> discuss   laugh   sing   talk   think

Dear Danny,

I'm sorry you were upset earlier today in music class. I'm embarrassed because when you were about to sing, Eva and I ¹_____ to each other pretty loudly. Then you ²_____ really well and we ³_____, but only because it was a funny song. Anyway, at a meeting yesterday, we ⁴_____ our band. We decided we need a lead singer and, of course, the whole time we ⁵_____ of you. Would you like to be our singer? Please say yes!

Emily

5 Write past continuous questions for the answers.

1 Why _____?

She was feeling nervous because she had an exam.

2 What _____?

They were talking about their new project.

3 Who _____?

He was visiting his grandparents.

4 Where _____?

I was camping in Costa Rica.

5 Why _____?

We were running because we were late.

6 How long _____?

She was waiting for more than an hour.

6 Complete the sentences with the simple past or past continuous form of the verbs in parentheses.

1 While we _____ (wait) for our friends, we _____ (start) to make tea.

2 He _____ (hear) an announcement while he _____ (sit) on the train.

3 Someone _____ (call) you while you _____ (take) a shower.

4 When their parents _____ (return), a band _____ (play) in their garage.

5 When the movie _____ (end), everyone in the theater _____ (cry).

6 While I _____ (look) for my shoes, I _____ (find) an old sandwich under my bed.

CUMULATIVE GRAMMAR

7 Complete the conversation with the missing words. (Circle) the correct options.

JAKE   Hi, Bella! Are you OK? When I ¹_____ you yesterday, you looked really upset.

BELLA There were ²_____ problems at home.

JAKE   That's too ³_____. What happened? Did you have a lot of homework?

BELLA No, I ⁴_____. But I was angry with my little brother.

JAKE   Really? What ⁵_____?

BELLA Oh, he ⁶_____ awful noisy video games all evening.

JAKE   My sister ⁷_____ playing those, too. What was the problem?

BELLA Well, he was making a terrible noise while I ⁸_____ my favorite show.

JAKE   Come on, Bella. Sometimes it can be difficult to play video games ⁹_____.

BELLA I never ¹⁰_____ video games!

JAKE   OK, so what ¹¹_____ in the end?

BELLA Well, in the end, I ¹²_____ Billy's game and hid it in a very secret place … in the kitchen.

JAKE   You're kidding!

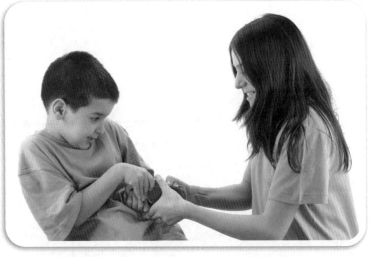

1 a seeing   b was seeing   c saw

2 a any   b some   c a

3 a bad   b well   c badly

4 a did   b do   c didn't

5 a did he do   b did he   c he did

6 a plays   b playing   c was playing

7 a loves   b is loving   c doesn't love

8 a watch   b was watching   c watched

9 a quietly   b quieter   c quiet

10 a am playing   b to play   c play

11 a happened   b was happening   c happens

12 a was taking   b take   c took

4 What do you value most?

VOCABULARY
Money Verbs

1 ⭐ Put the letters in the correct order to make money verbs.

1 s o t c   _cost_

2 n e h g c a   _____

3 r n a e   _____

4 r o o r w b   _____

5 e p n d s   _____

6 l e s l   _____

7 y a p   _____

8 d l n e   _____

9 v a e s   _____

10 e o w   _____

2 ⭐ Circle the correct options.

1 Save / Spend your money for something you really want.

2 Please can you borrow / lend me $5?

3 How much did that phone sell / cost you?

4 Harry earns / spends $2.50 when he washes his mom's car.

5 I don't like changing / owing my friends money.

6 She sold / bought her old bike to a friend from school.

3 ⭐ Complete the sentences with the words in the box.

change   cost   ~~earn~~   pay   sell   spend

1 You _earn_ money for work you do.

2 How much did those cool sneakers _____?

3 Can we _____ for our food with dollars on the plane?

4 Supermarkets _____ many different things to their customers.

5 Where can I _____ my Brazilian reais into dollars?

6 Don't _____ all your birthday money on video games and candy!

4 ⭐⭐ Complete the text messages with money verbs from Exercise 1.

> I can't ¹ _pay_ for my phone this month. Can I ² _____ $10 from you, please?

> But you ³ _____ me $5 from last month! ☹ I can't ⁴ _____ you any more. Sorry.

> What can I do? It's impossible to ⁵ _____ money – I never have any left at the end of the week.

> You can ⁶ _____ me your skateboard for $15. ☺

> My skateboard ⁷ _____ $50 when I bought it!

> Oh, well. Sorry, I can't help you then.

5 ⭐⭐ Complete the definitions with the correct form of the similar words in each pair.

1 You _lend_ some money to a friend. Your friend _____ money from you. (borrow / lend)

2 A sales assistant _____ something to you. You _____ something from a sales assistant. (buy / sell)

3 People _____ money for things they need later. They _____ money in a store or online. (save / spend)

4 You _____ money when you work. You _____ money in a competition or a lottery. (earn / win)

Explore It! 🖱

True or false?

In the U.S.A., they print more *Monopoly* money than real dollars every year.

Find another interesting fact about bills or coins. Write a question and send it to a classmate in an email, or ask them in the next class.

READING
A Newspaper Article

1 ⭐ Read the article. Which opinion in the last paragraph do you agree with? _____

Goodbye to Weekend Jobs?

Fifty years ago, it was very common for a North American teenager to work part-time. These days, the number of teens with a weekend job is falling.

The most common jobs in the U.S.A. for young people are working in stores and restaurants. In the past, teens could easily get these jobs.

One reason for the fall in part-time teenage workers is that, in the past, they could have a part-time job and do their schoolwork. Now, success on exams is the most important thing, and there's more pressure to do well in school.

"Working part-time and doing well in school isn't easy," says 15-year-old sales assistant Cheryl Bates. "You need to organize your time and maybe do

some of your homework at lunchtime. It's harder than you think, but when I earn my own money, I feel more independent because I don't need to ask my parents to buy me things."

Fourteen-year-old server Martin Cox adds, "Having a job is the best way to learn the skills you need for the future. I was the quietest boy in my

class, and I couldn't talk to people very well. Now, because I talk to customers at work, I'm much better in social situations."

So, can part-time work help to prepare young people for adult life, or does it put extra pressure on teens with already busy lives? What do you think?

2 ⭐⭐ Read the article again and check the meaning of the words in the box in a dictionary. Then complete the sentences.

> common   employer   ~~independent~~
> part-time   pressure

1 Maisie is a very _independent_ girl. She never needs much help.

2 Is there a lot of _____ to do well on all your exams at your school?

3 Fruit picking is usually a _____ job in the summer months. It's a very _____ job in a lot of countries.

4 Mrs. Preston is a good _____. All her teenage workers really like her.

3 ⭐⭐ Read the article again. Are the sentences *T* (true) or *F* (false)?

1 In the U.S.A., there weren't many young part-time workers in the past. ___F___

2 Many teenagers work in restaurants. ___

3 There was more pressure to do well in school in the past. ___

4 Cheryl thinks earning her own money is easy. ___

5 For Martin, talking to people isn't a problem now. ___

4 ⭐⭐⭐ Answer the questions with your own ideas.

1 Is part-time work for teenagers common in your country? Why / Why not?

_____

2 How do you get the money to buy the things you want?

_____

GRAMMAR IN ACTION
Could

1 ⭐ **Match 1–6 with a–f.**

1 I had no money,   [e]
2 Sara couldn't lend me $10   [ ]
3 All the lights in the store went out,   [ ]
4 Mozart could play and write music   [ ]
5 My dad could run marathons   [ ]
6 The bank was closed,   [ ]

a because she didn't have any money.
b so they couldn't change their money.
c from the age of four.
d and we couldn't see anything.
e so I couldn't buy anything.
f when he was younger.

2 ⭐⭐ **Write sentences that are true for you when you were six. Use the pictures.**

One, two, three … eight, nine, ten

100 meters

1 When I was six, I couldn't ride a bike.
2 _____
3 _____
4 _____
5 _____
6 _____

Comparative and Superlative Adjectives

3 ⭐ **Circle the correct options.**

1 The movie was (more exciting) / *the most exciting* than the book.
2 Samir was *happier* / *the happiest* in his old job than he is now.
3 Money isn't *more important* / *the most important* thing in life.
4 It was *more difficult* / *the most difficult* decision for him to make.
5 Today's class was *shorter* / *the shortest* than yesterday's.
6 The sales assistants were *more helpful* / *the most helpful* than they usually are.

4 ⭐⭐ **Put the words in the correct order to make sentences.**

1 yesterday / than / was / It's / today / it / hotter / .
   It's hotter today than it was yesterday.
2 mine / phone / than / your / Was / expensive / more / ?
   _____
3 worse / What's / than / your / losing / wallet / ?
   _____
4 quietest / town / Monday / the / is / in / day / .
   _____
5 are / cheapest / store / the / jeans / These / in / the / .
   _____
6 best / life / Yesterday / of / the / my / day / was / .
   _____

5 ⭐⭐ **Complete the text with the comparative or superlative form of the adjectives in the box.**

> exciting   expensive   ~~famous~~   old   rich   successful

I got some money for my birthday, so I bought a ticket to a City game. Everyone knows City: they're ¹ the most famous soccer team in the world. I think they're ² _____ than the other clubs in the UK because my great-grandfather was a City fan when he was a kid, and that was a long time ago! And they have a lot of money, so they're definitely ³ _____. They play fast and score lots of goals, so they're ⁴ _____ to watch than other teams. I also think they are ⁵ _____ team because they win most of their games. The only bad thing is that I can't go to every game because the tickets are probably ⁶ _____ tickets in the world.

VOCABULARY AND LISTENING

Caring Jobs

1 ⭐ **Complete the crossword. Use the clues.**

Across

1 A ... helps old or sick people in their homes.

3 A ... gives advice to people about the law.

4 A ... takes care of swimmers.

6 A ... helps to protect people from crime.

7 A ... does operations in hospitals.

8 A ... cares for sick people in hospitals.

10 A ... teaches very young children.

Down

2 A ... takes away the things we don't want.

5 A ... rescues people from dangerous situations.

6 A ... gives medical help to people before they get to a hospital.

9 A ... is a doctor for animals.

Put the gray letters in the correct order to complete this clue: A _____ works for no money.

2 ⭐ (Circle) the correct answers.

1 The (lifeguard) / firefighter told us not to swim there.

2 When our dog was sick, we took it to the vet / lawyer.

3 The paramedic / police officer stopped the motorcycle because it was going very fast.

4 The firefighter / garbage collector climbed into the burning house through a window.

5 My neighbor is a preschool teacher / caregiver in nursing home.

Monologues

🎧 **3** ⭐ **Listen to three people talking about their jobs. Which place connects all three speakers?** _____
4.01

🎧 **4** ⭐⭐ **Listen again and** (circle) **the correct answers.**
4.01

1 Speaker 1 ...

  a never has time for her family.

  (b) spent a long time studying.

  c doesn't spend much time working.

2 Speaker 1 ...

  a receives help from her team.

  b prefers working alone.

  c thinks the nurses need to work harder.

3 Speaker 2 ...

  a thinks his job is more important than a doctor's job.

  b didn't want to be a nurse when he was younger.

  c is doing the work he always wanted to do.

4 Speaker 2 thinks ...

  a some nurses are leaving because the job doesn't pay well.

  b it's sad that nurses want more money.

  c nurses need more responsibilities.

5 Speaker 3 does her job ...

  a on the weekend.   c three days a week.

  b in the morning.

5 ⭐⭐⭐ **Answer the questions in your notebook.**

1 Which job is the most tiring? Why?

2 Which job is the most important? Why?

GRAMMAR IN ACTION

Too, Too Much, Too Many

1 ⭐ **Complete the sentences with *too* and the words in the box.**

> busy   expensive   hard   hot   ~~tired~~   young

1 The nurses were ___too tired___ to go out after work.

2 The hospital parking lot costs $10. That's _____.

3 Is John _____ to stop working as a firefighter? He's 45.

4 It was _____ in the sun, so I went inside.

5 Can you help me this morning, or are you _____?

6 They couldn't answer the question because it was _____.

2 ⭐ (Circle) **the correct options.**

1 The doctor gave us too (much) / *many* information when she called.

2 Were there too *much* / *many* people in the waiting room?

3 Most caregivers say they have too *much* / *many* work.

4 Don't put too *much* / *many* milk in my coffee, please.

5 Is it possible to have too *much* / *many* good ideas?

6 Do you think surgeons earn too *much* / *many* money?

3 ⭐⭐ **Complete the conversation with *too*, *too much*, or *too many*.**

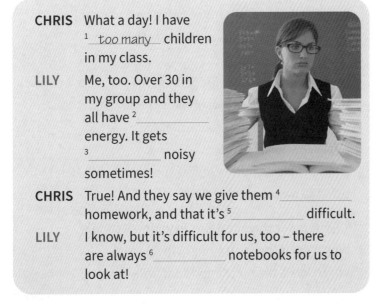

CHRIS What a day! I have ¹ _too many_ children in my class.

LILY Me, too. Over 30 in my group and they all have ² _____ energy. It gets ³ _____ noisy sometimes!

CHRIS True! And they say we give them ⁴ _____ homework, and that it's ⁵ _____ difficult.

LILY I know, but it's difficult for us, too – there are always ⁶ _____ notebooks for us to look at!

(Not) Enough + Noun

4 ⭐⭐ **Put the words in the correct order to make sentences.**

1 enough / don't / Doctors / money / nurses / and / earn / .

   Doctors and nurses don't earn enough money.

2 food / everyone / the / There / for / enough / is / in / world / .

   _____

3 volunteers / Are / organization / enough / your / in / there / ?

   _____

4 moment / enough / We / at / information / don't / have / the / .

   _____

5 in / Is / enough / classroom / space / this / there / ?

   _____

5 ⭐⭐ <u>Underline</u> **and correct one mistake in each sentence.**

1 Soccer players earn too <u>many</u> money, in my opinion. _____much_____

2 It's too noise in here for me; please be quiet. _____

3 The teacher gave us too much options to think about. _____

4 There wasn't information enough on the poster. _____

5 She was much young to be a caregiver. _____

6 ⭐⭐ **Complete the text about a dream job with *too*, *too much*, *too many*, or *(not) enough*.**

My dream job is to be a paramedic. Everyone knows that there are ¹ _n't enough_ doctors, but ² _____ people forget about the paramedics. I don't want to spend ³ _____ time studying when I finish school, and you don't need to take ⁴ _____ exams in emergency medicine to do it. But of course, you need to take some exams, and you need to be a good driver. When the roads are ⁵ _____ full of cars, you need ⁶ _____ driving skills to get to the hospital safely and quickly!

WRITING
An Opinion Essay

1 ⭐ **Read David's essay. Does he agree with the statement?**

It's good to have a weekend job while you're still in school. Do you agree?
By David Rodríguez

1 Nowadays, things cost a lot, and you need enough money to buy them. With a weekend job, you can earn your own money, but ¹ <u>in my opinion</u> , it's not a good idea.

2 ² _____ , working in a supermarket or café can sometimes be boring. Also, a student often gets lower pay than an adult for the same type of job. Perhaps because of this, more students get these jobs, and there isn't enough work for older people with families who need money more than you.

3 Also, teenagers usually sleep longer and get up later on weekends. ³ _____ that when you study hard at school all week, you need to relax on the weekend. I also think that enjoying free-time activities is more important than earning money.

4 ⁴ _____ , students need enough time for schoolwork, relaxing, and doing free-time activities. ⁵ _____ it's better to rest on the weekend and spend more time doing your favorite things. We'll have enough time for work when we're older!

2 ⭐ **Complete the essay with the phrases in the box.**

> First of all   I believe that   In conclusion
> ~~in my opinion~~   Personally, I think

3 ⭐⭐ **Read the essay again and answer the questions.**

1 What examples of part-time jobs does David give?

_____

2 In David's opinion, why can part-time jobs for teens be a problem for adults?

_____

3 According to David, what do teenagers typically do on weekends?

_____

4 What does David say is more important than money?

_____

4 ⭐ **Match the paragraphs (1–4) with the summaries (a–d).**

a a first reason for your opinion ☐

b a summary of your opinion ☐

c an introduction to the topic and your opinion ☐

d a second reason for your opinion ☐

PLAN

5 ⭐⭐ **Write an opinion essay. Choose one of the following topics or use David's topic. Take notes for each paragraph.**

> Weekend jobs teach you the skills you need for the future.
> Hard-working teachers don't earn enough money.

1 Introduce the topic and give your opinion:

_____

2 Give a reason for your opinion:

_____

3 Give a second reason:

_____

4 Summarize your opinion:

_____

WRITE

6 ⭐⭐⭐ **Write your opinion essay. Remember to include (*not*) *enough* and *too*, *too much*, *too many*, and the phrases from the *Useful Language* box (see Student's Book, p53).**

CHECK

7 Do you …
- have four paragraphs?
- give reasons for your opinions?
- summarize your opinion at the end?

VOCABULARY

1 Match 1–8 with a–h.

1 Henry lent his sister ☐
2 How much did you ☐
3 I borrowed $5 more from Ben, ☐
4 You can earn more money ☐
5 Are you saving money ☐
6 Do they sell ☐
7 How much does it cost ☐
8 I spend a lot of money ☐

a for anything special?
b when you work more hours.
c on presents for my friends.
d to change money here?
e pay for those tickets?
f so now I owe him $10.
g jeans in this store?
h some money for her lunch.

2 Circle the correct options.

1 *preschool teacher / paramedic*

2 *caregiver / lifeguard*

3 *vet / lifeguard*

4 *garbage collector / surgeon*

5 *nurse / volunteer*

6 *lawyer / police officer*

GRAMMAR IN ACTION

3 Complete the sentences with *could* or *couldn't*.

1 In the 1970s, people _____ send texts.
2 Roads were safer 50 years ago, so my grandpa _____ walk to school.
3 He _____ cycle because he didn't have a bike.
4 My great-grandma _____ play soccer because it was only for boys in those days.
5 My mom _____ play lots of sports at school. She played tennis, basketball, and volleyball.
6 Teenagers in 1950 _____ watch streaming series because there weren't any.

4 Complete the conversation with the comparative or superlative form of the adjectives in parentheses.

PABLO Hey, Laura. What's up?
LAURA My exam scores were
¹_____ (bad) than last time.
PABLO Oh, no. And your parents were
²_____ (angry) than usual, right?
LAURA Right. Dad was ³_____ (worried) about them than Mom, but I think I was the ⁴_____ (upset).
PABLO I can understand that. You're the ⁵_____ (hardworking) student in the class.
LAURA Thanks, but I think you're a ⁶_____ (hard) worker than me.
PABLO OK, we both work hard. But doing well on exams is ⁷_____ (difficult) than parents think. It isn't the ⁸_____ (easy) thing in the world!

5 Complete the conversation with *too, too much, too many,* or *(not) enough.*

PAT   Can you come swimming today? It's not ¹_____ busy on Sunday mornings.

JAMES Sorry, I can't. I don't have ²_____ time.

PAT   Really? We don't have ³_____ homework this weekend, only a little bit.

JAMES No, but I have ⁴_____ jobs to do at home.

PAT   Why do you need to do jobs?

JAMES I don't have ⁵_____ money, so my parents pay me to help with the chores on Sundays.

PAT   Well, I need more money, too, but I'm ⁶_____ lazy to do any extra work!

CUMULATIVE GRAMMAR

6 Complete the conversation with the missing words. (Circle) the correct options.

FRAN   Excuse me, I ¹_____ older people for my school magazine. Can you answer a few questions, please?

NIGEL Sure. I hope you don't have ²_____ difficult questions for me.

FRAN   No, don't worry! The first question is the ³_____ – do you still work?

NIGEL Well, I ⁴_____ as a firefighter for many years, but I'm retired now.

FRAN   I see. So now what ⁵_____ every day? Do you like reading or doing sudoku?

NIGEL Certainly not! I have ⁶_____ energy to sit around all day.

FRAN   You're ⁷_____ my grandparents, then, because that's all they do!

NIGEL Of course I enjoy my free time, but I get ⁸_____ bored when I do nothing.

FRAN   So are there ⁹_____ special things you do, now that you're not working?

NIGEL I'm a volunteer at ¹⁰_____ outdoor activity center, where I give talks about being safe.

FRAN   That's great! In my opinion, ¹¹_____ retired people share their skills.

NIGEL Very true. It's definitely the ¹²_____ way to stay active and healthy! Next question?

1 a interviewed   b 'm interviewing   c I was interviewing

2 a too much   b too many   c enough

3 a most easy   b easy   c easiest

4 a was work   b working   c worked

5 a do you do   b did you do   c are you doing

6 a much   b enough   c too much

7 a fittest than   b fitter than   c fittest that

8 a too   b too much   c not enough

9 a much   b an   c any

10 a some   b a   c an

11 a not enough   b much   c not much

12 a good   b better   c best

5 What is your dream house?

VOCABULARY
Furniture

1 ⭐ **Look at the photos and complete the furniture words.**

1 a r m c h a i r
2 c _ _ _ _ _ o _
  d _ _ _ _ _ _ _
3 c _ _ _ _ _ _ _
4 s _ _ _ _ _ _ _
5 p _ _ _ _ _ _ _
6 b _ _ _ _ _ _ _ _
7 d _ _ _ _
8 f _ _ _ _ _
9 c _ _ _ _ _ _ _
10 w _ _ _ _ _ _ _ _
11 c _ _ _ _ _ _
12 f _ _ _ _ _
13 s _ _ _ _

2 ⭐ **Circle the correct options to complete the text.**

I love my bedroom and spend a lot of time in it. There's a nice warm ¹*cupboard* / *carpet* on the ²*floor* / *ceiling*, and I have a comfortable old ³*chest of drawers* / *armchair* by the window where I can sit and read. In the corner, there is a ⁴*desk* / *sink* where I do my homework, and above it are some ⁵*shelves* / *pictures* of my friends and family. I have a big ⁶*fridge* / *wardrobe* for my clothes, but I sometimes leave them on my bed!

3 ⭐⭐ **Complete the sentences with words from Exercise 1.**

1 Sheila is very tall, so she can touch the _____*ceiling*_____ in her bedroom.
2 Aunt Adie has an old _____ of her grandparents on the wall.
3 He keeps his smaller clothes, like socks and T-shirts, in a _____.
4 Don't come in with dirty shoes. I cleaned the kitchen _____ this morning.
5 You can find tea and coffee in that _____ next to the window.
6 We brush our teeth in the bathroom _____.

Explore It! 🖱️

Guess the correct answer.

The biggest hotel in Europe is the Izmailovo Hotel in Moscow. It has *3,500* / *7,500* / *9,500* beds.

Find another interesting fact about a hotel. Write a question and send it to a classmate in an email, or ask them in the next class.

READING
A Magazine Article

1 ★★ Read the article. In your opinion, which is the best place to live in? _____

No Place Like Home

In this week's edition of *City Life*, we asked two 13-year-olds about living in London. What do they like about where they live? Is there anything they don't like?

"I live in an apartment building in Wembley, in the northwest of London. It has 21 floors! I live on the second to top floor. City life isn't as quiet as life in the country, but it's very quiet so high up, and the views are amazing. I can see Wembley soccer stadium from my bedroom window, and I can sometimes hear the crowd when they score a goal! We live near a canal, and I can cycle to school in five minutes along the canal path. It's great to live here. I only think my apartment isn't as good as a house when the elevator doesn't work!"

Kelly

"I live in a row of houses in a part of London called Camden. It takes me about ten minutes to walk to school from home. There's a famous market nearby called Camden Market. It's very popular with street musicians – and tourists, of course! The houses on my street are all painted different colors, but I don't like that very much. I think it's too colorful! My room is on the top floor of my house. The ceiling isn't as high as I'd like, but the room is big enough for just me. From my window, I can watch the boats and barges go by on the Regent's Canal at the end of our yard. I love living in my house."

Hasan

2 ★★ Read the article again and check the meaning of these words in a dictionary. Then complete the sentences.

> barge   canal   crowd   ~~floor~~   path   row

1 We stayed on the top ____*floor*____ of an apartment building in New York.
2 We sat in the front _____ of chairs during the class presentations.
3 My Dutch friend lives in a houseboat on a _____ .
4 A type of boat called a _____ transports things along rivers and canals.
5 To get to the village, follow this _____ .
6 There was a big _____ of people outside of the concert.

3 ★★ (Circle) the correct answers.

1 *City Life* magazine asked Kelly and Hasan about … in London.
 a cycling   (c) living
 b going to school
2 Kelly lives on the … floor.
 a 20th   b 21st   c 2nd
3 She likes … .
 a living high up   c walking to school
 b watching soccer
4 Hasan's house is close to … .
 a a market   c the country
 b Wembley
5 He doesn't like the … on his street.
 a tourists   c colorful houses
 b musicians
6 From his bedroom, he can see … .
 a market stalls   c colorful houses
 b boats and barges

4 ★★★ Answer the questions with your own ideas.

1 How are the houses in the article similar to your house?

_____

2 Name one good thing and one bad thing about living in a tall building.

_____

GRAMMAR IN ACTION
(Not) As + Adjective + As

1 ⭐ **Complete the sentences with the adjective in parentheses and (not) as … as. Then check your answers in the article on page 41.**

1 Hasan is ___as happy as___ (happy) Kelly with his home.
2 Kelly thinks country life is _____ (noisy) life in the city.
3 Kelly's trip to school is _____ (slow) Hasan's trip.
4 Hasan is _____ (old) Kelly.
5 The house is _____ (tall) the apartment building.
6 The apartment building is _____ (colorful) the houses in Camden.

2 ⭐⭐ **Look at the information and complete the sentences with is (not) as … as and an adjective from the box.**

> big   busy   ~~expensive~~   fast   good   old

1 Tim's ticket = $10.00 / Liz's ticket = $12.00
  Tim's ticket _isn't as expensive as_ Liz's ticket.
2 house = 200 meters / apartment = 200 meters
  The apartment _____ the house.
3 Juan's English exam = 8 out of 10 / Olivia's English exam = 8 out of 10
  Olivia's exam score _____ Juan's exam score.
4 Saturday's market = 200 shoppers / Monday's market = 50 shoppers
  The Monday market _____ the Saturday market.
5 a letter = two days / an email = two seconds
  A letter _____ an email.
6 Luke = 15 years old / Nick = 15 years old
  Luke _____ Nick.

(Not) + Adjective + Enough

3 ⭐ **Complete the sentences with the adjectives in the box.**

> ~~fit~~   hot   old   safe   well

1 I'd love to be __fit__ enough to run a marathon, but I'm not.
2 See the red flag? The water here isn't _____ enough to swim in.
3 The soup isn't _____ enough. It needs five more minutes.
4 When are you _____ enough to drive a car in your country?
5 He was in the hospital, and he's still not _____ enough to go to school.

4 ⭐ **Match 1–6 with a–f.**

1 You can take a shower [d]
2 This puzzle is too easy [ ]
3 Can I have some sugar, please? [ ]
4 We didn't understand because [ ]
5 He tried to park his car, [ ]
6 Her new coat is [ ]

a nice enough for the party.
b My coffee isn't sweet enough.
c the instructions weren't clear enough.
d when the water is warm enough.
e because the clues aren't hard enough.
f but the space wasn't wide enough.

5 ⭐⭐ **Complete the conversation with the phrases in the box.**

> as comfortable as   as expensive as   as nice as
> as tall as   ~~long enough~~   soft enough

SARA Here's a furniture store. Can we look for a new bed for me, Mom? My old bed isn't ¹ _long enough_ for me anymore.

MOM I know, you're nearly ² _____ me now! OK, what about this bed?

SARA Mmm, it isn't ³ _____ for me – it's too hard. It isn't ⁴ _____ the one I have now!

MOM Look! This one isn't ⁵ _____ that one – it's a better price, and it's the right size.

SARA But it's not ⁶ _____ the first one. I'm not sure about the color. Oh, I can't decide, Mom!

VOCABULARY AND LISTENING
Household Chores

1 ⭐ (Circle) the correct verbs to complete the household chores.

1 (mop) / *make* the floor
2 *make* / *do* the ironing
3 *do* / *make* the bed
4 *empty* / *dust* the furniture
5 *load* / *make* the dishwasher
6 *make* / *do* the dishes
7 *load* / *sweep* the floor
8 *empty* / *vacuum* the carpet
9 *do* / *make* the laundry

2 ⭐ Match the photos with six of the phrases from Exercise 1.

1   do the ironing

2 _____

3 _____

4 _____

5 _____

6 _____

🎧 **3** ⭐ Listen to an interview about how a family shares the chores at home. Who helps more: Daisy or Milo?
5.01

_____

🎧 **4** ⭐⭐ Listen again and (circle) the correct options.
5.01

1 Daisy doesn't like (mopping the floor) / *dusting the furniture*.
2 Milo does the *laundry* / *dishes* on the weekend.
3 His parents *pay* / *thank* him for helping out with the chores.
4 The children's father does *all* / *some* of the cleaning.
5 Their mother *likes* / *doesn't like* cooking.
6 Milo and Daisy do *the dishes* / *their homework* after dinner.

5 ⭐⭐⭐ Answer the questions.

1 What do you do to help out at home?

_____

2 Who cooks in your family?

_____

3 What chores do you like or hate doing? Why?

_____

GRAMMAR IN ACTION
Have To

1 ☆ (Circle) the correct options.

1 I really (have to) / don't have to clean up my room because I can't find anything.

2 Pat has to / doesn't have to cycle to school because it's too far for her to walk there.

3 Most children have to / don't have to go to school on Sundays.

4 You have to / don't have to wash those jeans. They're clean.

5 There's no bread, so you have to / don't have to buy more.

2 ☆☆ Complete the sentences with the correct form of *have to* and the verb in parentheses.

1 Jake ___has to run___ (run) when he's late for school.

2 You _____ (make) your bed because I don't have time.

3 We _____ (shop) for food because Dad does that.

4 My three-year-old sister _____ (do) anything to help around the house. She's too young.

5 I _____ (wash) the car because we don't have one.

6 Bill _____ (help) his parents when they're too busy to do everything.

3 ☆☆ Put the words in the correct order to make questions.

1 shop / day / dad / Does / to / have / every / your / ?
   Does your dad have to shop every day?

2 help / house / have / Do / around / you / to / the / ?
   _____

3 the / have / sleep / outside / Does / dog / to / ?
   _____

4 carpet / vacuum / have / Do / to / you / the / ?
   _____

5 children / bed / to / have / be / in / by / Do / nine / the / ?
   _____

6 Owen / Does / to / have / leave / breakfast / before / ?
   _____

4 ☆☆ Look at the chart and complete the sentences with the correct form of *have to*.

	Tom	Lisa	Mike
Do the dishes	✗	✓	✗
Do the laundry	✗	✓	✗
Mop the kitchen floor	✗	✗	✗
Vacuum the carpet	✓	✗	✗
Make breakfast	✓	✗	✗
Make our beds	✓	✓	✓

1 Lisa ___has to do___ the dishes and the laundry.

2 Tom, Lisa, and Mike _____ the kitchen floor.

3 Mike's very little so he _____ much.

4 Mike only _____ his bed.

5 Tom _____ the carpet, but he _____ the dishes.

6 Tom _____ breakfast.

5 ☆☆☆ Complete the text with the correct form of *have to* and the verbs in the box.

| carry   clean up   do |
| mop   put   take   ~~work~~ |

My younger sister, Jenny, [1] *doesn't have to work* very hard at school because she's still little, but she and her classmates [2] _____ the classroom at the end of the day so it's clean. They [3] _____ their chairs on top of their desks, but they [4] _____ the floor, of course – the custodian [5] _____ that. Jenny has some heavy books, but she [6] _____ them home every day – she can keep them in the classroom. When there's homework, Jenny brings the book that she needs home, but she [7] _____ it back to school the next day. She's a very good student!

WRITING

A Description of a House

1 ⭐ **Look at the photos and read the description. Which house does it describe: a or b?** _____

> **1** This vacation home is in a quiet place with great views, but it's ¹(also) / too close enough to a big town. You can drive to the stores, and there's a bus, ²as well as / too.
>
> **2** The house is a long, modern building with four huge bedrooms upstairs. The living room has big windows, but the windows upstairs are big ³as well / as well as. There's a beautiful tropical garden, and there are plants on the balcony, ⁴as well as / too.
>
> **3** One very special thing about this house is the home movie theater. It's not as big as a real theater, but you don't have to leave the house! It's really cool because ⁵as well as / also seats for ten people, there's a fridge and a cupboard for yummy snacks! It's the best vacation home in the world!
>
> _Daniel Bell (13), Los Angeles_

2 ⭐ (Circle) the correct options (1–5) in the description.

3 ⭐⭐ **Read the description again. Are the sentences _T_ (true) or _F_ (false)?**
1 The house is in the center of a big town.   _F_
2 There's no public transportation near the house.   ___
3 There are big windows upstairs.   ___
4 The house is special because there's a movie theater in it.   ___

4 ⭐ **Match headings a–c with paragraphs 1–3.**
a What does the house have? ☐
b What is really special about the house? ☐
c Where is the house? ☐

PLAN
5 ⭐⭐ **Write a description of a vacation home. Find a photo of a vacation home online or in a magazine. Take notes about these things.**
1 Where the vacation home is:

_____

Why you like it:

_____

2 What rooms, furniture, and other things it has:

_____

3 Why the vacation home is special:

_____

WRITE
6 ⭐⭐⭐ **Write your description. Remember to include adjectives with (_not_) as … as, _enough_, and _have to/don't have to_, and the phrases from the _Useful Language_ box (see Student's Book p65).**

CHECK
7 Do you …
- have three paragraphs?
- describe what the vacation house has?
- explain why the vacation home is special?

VOCABULARY

1 (Circle) the correct options.

1 Ellie is sitting in a comfortable *carpet / armchair* and reading a graphic novel.

2 Take the cups out of the dishwasher and put them in the *cupboard / fridge*.

3 After he irons his shirts, Tom puts them carefully in his *desk / wardrobe*.

4 We need some more *shelves / carpets* above the sink in the bathroom.

5 Don't forget to clean the *floor / sink* after you brush your teeth.

6 There's milk all over the kitchen *ceiling / floor*. Did someone break a cup?

7 Mom has a special place in her *desk / chest of drawers* for scarves and gloves.

8 Berto was vacuuming the living room *shelves / carpet* when he found his lost key.

9 There's bread on the table and butter and cheese in the *fridge / sink*.

10 Ryan has a nice *desk / bookcase* in his room, but he never does his homework there.

2 Complete the household chores in the spidergram.

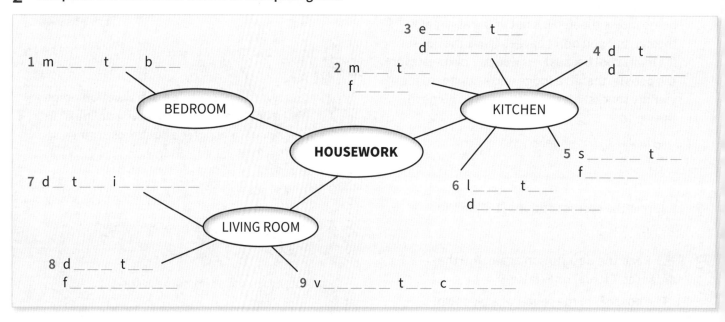

1 m _ _ _ _ t _ _ b _ _ _

BEDROOM

7 d _ t _ _ _ i _ _ _ _ _ _ _ _

8 d _ _ _ _ t _ _ _
f _ _ _ _ _ _ _ _ _

LIVING ROOM

HOUSEWORK

9 v _ _ _ _ _ _ t _ _ _ c _ _ _ _ _ _

2 m _ _ _ t _ _ _
f _ _ _ _ _

3 e _ _ _ _ _ _ t _ _ _
d _ _ _ _ _ _ _ _ _ _ _

KITCHEN

4 d _ _ t _ _ _
d _ _ _ _ _ _ _

5 s _ _ _ _ _ _ t _ _
f _ _ _ _ _

6 l _ _ _ _ t _ _
d _ _ _ _ _ _ _ _ _ _

GRAMMAR IN ACTION

3 Rewrite the sentences with (*not*) *as … as* or (*not*) *enough* and the adjectives in parentheses.

1 Your house is the same size as my house. (big)

Your house _____ .

2 The weather is warmer today. (cold)

The weather today _____ .

3 Sam is more nervous than Jack. (relaxed)

Sam _____ .

4 Nicky is too young to watch that movie. (old)

Nicky _____ .

5 I don't need a bigger desk than this one. (big)

This desk _____ .

6 Frank is stronger than his brother. (strong)

Frank's brother _____ .

7 Is there enough sugar in your coffee? (sweet)

Is your coffee _____ ?

8 Sofia and her mother are 1.62 meters tall. (tall)

Sofia _____ .

4 Complete the sentences with the correct form of *have to*.

1 We _____ do the dishes by hand. We have a dishwasher.

2 You _____ put the cups on the top shelf, not on the bottom.

3 Lisa _____ help in the yard. Her dad does that.

4 We _____ wash our clothes by hand. We use the washing machine.

5 You _____ give me a fork. I can use chopsticks.

6 Mr. Kelly _____ clean the school windows. That's his job.

7 You _____ help me, but thanks. I know what to do.

8 They _____ buy a new vacuum cleaner. Their old one broke.

CUMULATIVE GRAMMAR

5 Complete the conversation with the missing words. (Circle) the correct options.

DAD	Hey, Kevin, come over here. I ¹_____ at some vacation websites.
KEVIN	Oh, great. Can I take the tent you ²_____ me for my birthday?
DAD	Well, your mom ³_____ camping.
KEVIN	Oh, but Dad, tents are ⁴_____ these days than they were in the past.
DAD	Yes, but I ⁵_____ about a vacation home, you know, with a pool.
KEVIN	A vacation home isn't ⁶_____ a campsite, Dad.
DAD	⁷_____ where we stayed last summer?
KEVIN	Yeah, it was nice, but it wasn't ⁸_____ for me.
DAD	A vacation home is definitely ⁹_____ .
KEVIN	Yeah, but it's boring. There aren't ¹⁰_____ other kids to hang out with.
DAD	Well, I'm sorry your mother and I aren't ¹¹_____ for you, Kevin.
KEVIN	No, Dad, I didn't mean that. But you ¹²_____ agree: you're not as much fun as my friends!

	a	b	c
1	look	'm looking	do look
2	buy	buyed	bought
3	not like	doesn't like	don't like
4	better	good	best
5	were thinking	was thinking	did thought
6	as interesting as	more interesting as	interesting than
7	Are you liking	Were you liking	Did you like
8	enough exciting	very exciting enough	exciting enough
9	most comfortable as	more comfortable	the more comfortable
10	some	one	any
11	cooler enough	enough cool	cool enough
12	has to	don't have to	have to

6 How can I stay safe?

VOCABULARY
Accidents and Injuries

1 ⭐ Put the letters in the correct order to make words and phrases about accidents and injuries.

1 tge ttneib ___get bitten___
2 tih _____
3 usbrie _____
4 npsira _____
5 uct _____
6 tge gutsn _____
7 runb _____
8 lafl fof _____
9 psil _____
10 tarccsh _____
11 kebra _____
12 ptir vroe _____

2 ⭐ Circle the odd one out.

1 break / bruise / slip **your arm**
2 fall off / sprain / trip over **a bike**
3 get cut / get stung / get bitten **by an insect**
4 hit / break / bruise **your head on the door**

3 ⭐ Match 1–6 with a–f.

1 Jeremy got stung ☐ e
2 The bruise on my arm ☐
3 You can't play soccer ☐
4 I didn't see my bag, ☐
5 They were running around the pool ☐
6 He fell off his surfboard ☐

a and I tripped over it.
b if you break your leg.
c when they slipped on the wet floor.
d and into the ocean.
e on his leg by a bee.
f is now black and blue.

4 ⭐⭐ Complete the sentences with the correct form of the words and phrases from Exercise 1.

1 Henry ___sprained___ his ankle running for the bus.
2 The cat _____ my arm when I picked it up.
3 You can easily _____ your hand while cooking.
4 You can _____ by mosquitoes when you camp near water.
5 My grandma _____ her finger on a sharp knife.
6 He _____ his head as he was getting out of the car.

5 ⭐⭐ Complete the chat with the correct form of the words and phrases in the box.

> bruise   ~~fall off~~   hit   not break
> sprain   trip over

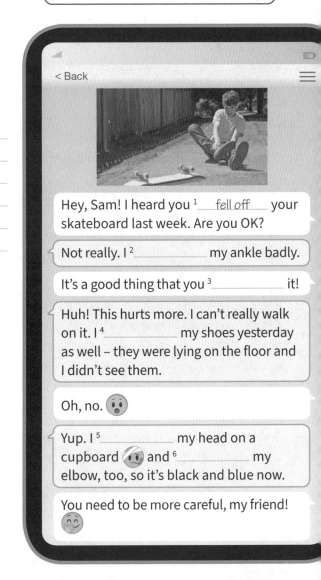

< Back

Hey, Sam! I heard you ¹___fell off___ your skateboard last week. Are you OK?

Not really. I ²_____ my ankle badly.

It's a good thing that you ³_____ it!

Huh! This hurts more. I can't really walk on it. I ⁴_____ my shoes yesterday as well – they were lying on the floor and I didn't see them.

Oh, no. 😲

Yup. I ⁵_____ my head on a cupboard 🤕 and ⁶_____ my elbow, too, so it's black and blue now.

You need to be more careful, my friend! 🤔

Explore It! 🖱

Guess the correct answer.

Both male and female / Only male / Only female mosquitoes bite humans.

Find another interesting fact about mosquitoes. Write a question and send it to a classmate in an email, or ask them in the next class.

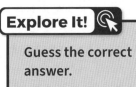

READING
An Online Article

1 ⭐ Read the article and write the headings in the correct places (1–4).

> Burns   Do Not Eat or Drink!   Falls   Things Up Noses

● ● ●

DANGER AT HOME!   HOME | **STORIES** | PHOTOS

1 _____

You probably think that the most dangerous room in the house is the kitchen, but in fact, most accidents happen in the living room! Small children can get serious burns from hot drinks or open fires. Candles are also the cause of many accidents in the living room – a candle near a curtain can start a horrible house fire!

2 _____

Many people go to the hospital after getting poisoned, especially young children. Do you sometimes paint your bedroom? When you finish painting a wall, put the paints in a safe place so that young children don't try to drink them. Medicines, too, should be in a top bathroom cupboard – they shouldn't be easy for kids to get.

3 _____

This is a surprising accident but also a common one. Young children often put the strangest things up their noses: frozen peas, crayons, fries … . They think it's funny, but it can be serious. These objects get stuck, and it sometimes requires a hospital visit to get them out.

4 _____

Falling is the most common accident in the home. Be careful: climbing up a ladder to get something down from a high shelf can be very risky. This happens most often to people over 65 and kids under 15. And remember: young children must not play near open windows – thousands of children fall out of them every year, so watch out.

2 ⭐⭐ Read the article again and check the meaning of these words in a dictionary. Then complete the sentences.

> candles   ladder   ~~medicine~~
> poison   risky   stuck

1 Judy was sick last year, and she's still taking a lot of __medicine__ .

2 My little brother had seven _____ on his birthday cake.

3 Drinking dirty or polluted water can _____ you.

4 It's very _____ to light a candle and leave it near a young child.

5 We needed a _____ to get the boxes down from the top shelf.

6 My hand got _____ under the sofa, and I couldn't get it out.

3 ⭐⭐ Read the article again. Answer the questions.

1 Which room is the most dangerous, according to the article?
   _____the living room_____

2 How can house fires start in the living room?
   _____

3 What's the best place to keep medicines?
   _____

4 Why do young children put things up their noses?
   _____

5 Which age groups have the most accidents with falls?
   _____

6 How can an open window be dangerous?
   _____

4 ⭐⭐⭐ Answer the questions with your own ideas.

1 Which fact in the article surprised you the most? Why?
   _____

2 Do you light candles at home? When?
   _____

GRAMMAR IN ACTION
Should/Shouldn't and *Must/Must Not*

1 ⭐ **Complete the sentences with *should* or *shouldn't*.**

1 You _____should_____ always be careful with candles.

2 You _____ leave a lighted candle in an empty room.

3 Dad says that we _____ clean our shoes.

4 Maybe we _____ have a smoke alarm in the classroom.

5 You _____ take other people's medicine.

6 We _____ prevent as many accidents as we can.

2 ⭐ **Complete the sentences with the words in the box.**

> should be   should do   should send
> shouldn't drink   shouldn't laugh   ~~shouldn't swim~~

1 There's a red flag on the beach, so you _shouldn't swim_ here.

2 My uncle had an accident at work. I _____ him a card.

3 It's very icy today, so you _____ careful that you don't slip.

4 Oliver got stung by a bee. You _____ at him – it's not funny!

5 My brother has a broken arm, so I _____ the dishes.

6 Hey, you _____ that! It's medicine, not fruit juice!

3 ⭐⭐ **Complete the poster with *should* or *shouldn't* and an appropriate verb.**

> ## Can't sleep at bedtime?
> ## Can't get up in the morning?
>
> **Here's some advice from SLEEP NURSE!**
>
> You ¹_____should do_____ exercise in the fresh air every day.
>
> You ²_____ tea or coffee in the evening.
>
> You ³_____ to quiet relaxing music.
>
> You ⁴_____ scary movies in bed.
>
> You ⁵_____ your phone in a different room.
>
> You ⁶_____ off your light before you go to sleep.

4 ⭐⭐ **Complete the sentences about the signs using *must* or *must not*. Sometimes there is more than one possible answer.**

1 You _must not park here_ .

2 You _____ .

3 You _____ .

4 You _____ .

5 You _____ .

6 You _____ .

5 ⭐⭐ (Circle) **the best options to complete the conversation.**

PAULA I think you ¹(*should*)/ *shouldn't* / *must* come to judo class, Lola. It's really fun!

LOLA Do you really think I ²*should* / *must* / *must not*? I'm not very athletic.

PAULA I know, but Mom says we ³*should* / *shouldn't* / *must* do at least one after-school activity, so you have to choose one.

LOLA OK, what are the rules? What do I need to know?

PAULA First, you ⁴*shouldn't* / *must* / *must not* be late because you can't come in once the class starts. Second, you ⁵*should* / *must* / *must not* bring judo clothes – you can't wear normal clothes. And the most important thing: you ⁶*should* / *must* / *must not* listen to everything the instructor says. Judo can be dangerous.

LOLA Mmm, it sounds kind of scary!

VOCABULARY AND LISTENING

Parts of the Body

A Radio Interview

1 ⭐ **Find 11 more words for parts of the body in the word search. The words can be in any direction.**

A	K	E	E	H	C	C	L	V
R	W	D	O	C	H	I	N	N
F	O	R	E	H	E	A	D	M
Y	B	K	J	T	S	F	K	E
U	L	C	P	E	T	M	N	C
L	E	E	H	E	X	Z	E	I
A	C	N	S	T	T	O	E	A
W	R	I	S	T	V	N	W	N
R	E	D	L	U	O	H	S	R

2 ⭐ (Circle) **the correct options.**

1 Marie's hair covered her (forehead) / neck, almost to her eyes.

2 The boys' *chins / cheeks* were red when they came in from the cold.

3 Joe walked on broken glass and cut his *wrist / heel*.

4 Our teacher wore a pretty, long scarf around her *neck / elbow*.

5 Olympic swimmers often have very wide *chests / elbows*.

6 The girl fell off her bike and bruised her *teeth / knee*.

7 Ballet dancers wear special shoes so they can dance on their *toes / elbows*.

8 She was wearing three gold bracelets around her *shoulder / wrist*.

🎧 3 6.01 ⭐ **Look at the pictures about a story. What do you think happened? Listen and put the pictures in the correct order (1–6).**

🎧 4 6.01 ⭐⭐ **Listen again. Are the sentences *T* (true) or *F* (false)?**

1 Toby was on the boat with a friend. _F_

2 Toby says dolphins can sometimes be dangerous. ___

3 The boys didn't know what the dolphins were doing. ___

4 The shark disappeared after about an hour. ___

5 One dolphin injured Toby's shoulder. ___

6 People can find more animal stories on the radio station's website. ___

5 ⭐⭐⭐ **Answer the questions with your own ideas.**

1 Which other animals are especially smart?

_____

2 Which other animals sometimes protect humans? How?

_____

GRAMMAR IN ACTION
Zero Conditional and First Conditional

1 ⭐ **Complete the zero conditional sentences with the correct form of the verbs in parentheses.**

1 People _don't swim_ (not swim) here when they ___see___ (see) the red flag on the beach.

2 When sharks _____ (get) hungry, they _____ (be) a danger to swimmers.

3 Broken glass _____ (cut) your skin if you _____ (touch) it.

4 Swimmers _____ (get) very cold if they _____ (stay) in the ocean too long.

5 If the temperature _____ (fall) below 0 °C, water _____ (turn) into ice.

6 If a bee _____ (sting) you, it really _____ (hurt).

2 ⭐⭐ **Write zero conditional sentences.**

1 if / I / drink coffee at night / I / not sleep well / .

If I drink coffee at night, I don't sleep well.

2 if / we / study hard / we / do well on our tests / .

_____

3 when / Helena / feel sick / she / not come to school / .

_____

4 my little brother / fall down / if / he / run too fast / .

_____

5 I / feel really bad / when / I / forget my friends' birthdays / .

_____

6 if / you / call the doctor after nine / nobody / answer / .

_____

3 ⭐⭐ **Complete the zero conditional sentences with the correct form of the verbs in the box.**

| break   die   eat   fall   get   go   ~~look~~   not rain   ~~swim~~   walk |

1 Ross always ___swims___ in the river if it ___looks___ safe.

2 Children _____ cavities in their teeth if they _____ too much sugar.

3 If it _____ all summer, enough plants and animals _____ .

4 Older people _____ down easily when they _____ on ice.

5 You _____ to the hospital if you _____ your leg.

4 ⭐⭐ **Circle the correct options.**

1 I'll carry your bags if your shoulders *will hurt* / *hurt*.

2 If your cat scratches Laura, she *isn't* / *won't be* happy.

3 The roads will be dangerous if it *snows* / *will snow* tonight.

4 There will be an accident if they *aren't* / *won't be* more careful.

5 If she *will run* / *runs* too fast, her chest will start to hurt.

5 ⭐⭐ **Complete the first conditional sentences in the text with the correct form of the verbs in parentheses.**

Don't Get Lost!

If you [1] ___walk___ (walk) a lot in the forest, it's possible that one day you [2] _____ (get) lost. If this happens, sit down and eat and drink something. If you [3] _____ (feel) calm, you [4] _____ (think) more clearly. Can you send a text or make a call? If you [5] _____ (make) contact with someone, [6] _____ you _____ (know) how to direct them to where you are? If you [7] _____ (look) around, you [8] _____ probably _____ (recognize) something. Remember to always take the correct equipment so you don't get lost in the first place. You [9] _____ (be) better prepared if you [10] _____ (pack) a map and a compass before you go!

WRITING
A Blog Post

1 Read the blog post. Do you agree with the advice? _____

● ● ●

The Climbers' Climbing Blog

Thanks for reading my blog! Here are a few of my readers' questions and my answers.

I always bruise my knees and elbows when I'm rock climbing. What should I do to avoid that? *Spidergirl*

You should buy some knee and elbow pads. But [1] *make sure / that's why* that you climb in the correct way. You won't bruise anything if you're careful. [2] *If you ask me, / Make sure* you need some expert advice and maybe a lesson or two!

I'm 11, and I'd love to go climbing with my older brothers, but they say I'm too young. What's a good age to start climbing? *Katya*

If you're tall and strong enough, you'll be able to climb now! [3] *That's why / I'd say* it's safe to start climbing at your age if you start with small climbs and you have good climbers with you. If you're careful, you'll be fine. Enjoy!

When's the safest time to go climbing? I only climb in the summer, but I want to do more. *Barbara*

In the U.S.A., spring and summer are the best times. You'll slip and fall if you climb on wet rocks. [4] *Make sure / That's why* you shouldn't do it on rainy days. And of course, you must never climb in snowy or icy weather if you don't have special equipment.

That's all for now. Have fun, and happy climbing!

2 ⭐ (Circle) the correct options (1–4) in the blog post.

3 ⭐⭐ Read the blog post again. Write *S* (Spidergirl), *K* (Katya), or *B* (Barbara) for each sentence.

1 She wants to know the best time for climbing. ___

2 The blogger thinks she should have classes. ___

3 The blogger says she should go with other climbers. ___

4 ⭐⭐ Read the blog post again and (circle) the correct answers.

1 Rock climbers should wear knee and elbow pads to avoid … .

   (a) bruises   b falls   c climbing incorrectly

2 Katya's brothers think she's not … enough to start climbing.

   a tall   b old   c strong

3 Katya should start with … climbs.

   a good   b short   c careful

4 Barbara doesn't climb on … days.

   a sunny   b summer   c winter

5 Climbers need special equipment in … weather.

   a summer   b rainy   c icy

PLAN

5 ⭐⭐ Write a blog post to give safety advice. Choose an activity and think of three questions about doing it safely. Take notes for the answers in your notebook.

1 _____

2 _____

3 _____

WRITE

6 ⭐⭐⭐ Write your blog post. Remember to include an introduction, three questions and answers, an ending, and phrases from the *Useful Language* box (see Student's Book, p77).

CHECK

7 Do you …
- answer each question?
- use *should/shouldn't* and *must/must not*?
- use vocabulary from this unit?

VOCABULARY

1 Complete the crossword. Use the clues.

Across

2 You … on icy roads.

7 A … around your eye is called a "black eye."

9 You … … objects on the floor if you don't see them.

10 Don't … your hand in the fire!

12 She … her head on the cupboard door.

Down

1 It hurts a lot when you … your ankle.

3 Don't stand on the wall or you'll … … !

4 Rugby players often … their noses.

5 You can … … by a bee if you make it angry.

6 You can … … by mosquitoes if you leave the window open.

8 Does your cat sometimes … you?

11 He … his foot on a sharp rock.

2 Complete the words for parts of the body with the missing vowels.

1 f _ r _ h _ _ d

2 h _ _ l

3 _ l b _ w

4 k n _ _

5 ch _ n

6 n _ c k

7 ch _ st

8 sh _ _ l d _ r

9 ch _ _ k

10 t _ _ t h

11 w r _ st

12 t _ _

GRAMMAR IN ACTION

3 Are the <u>underlined</u> words correct in the sentences? Correct the incorrect ones.

1 You <u>must not</u> drive on the right on U.S. roads.
_____must_____

2 If she likes helping sick people, she <u>should</u> become a nurse. _____

3 You <u>must not</u> put metal in a microwave.
_____

4 Cyclists <u>must not</u> stop when they see a stop sign.
_____

5 Children <u>should</u> brush their teeth after eating candy. _____

6 You <u>must not</u> buy a ticket when you travel on public transportation. _____

7 You <u>should</u> go rock climbing in the rain. It's incredibly dangerous! _____

4 Put the words in the correct order to make conditional sentences. Add commas where necessary.

1 you get stung / it hurts / If / by a bee / .
_____

2 warm clothes / we wear / We won't get cold / if / .
_____

3 If / I won't / I see a red flag / go swimming / .
_____

4 be happy / you wake him up / if / Nikita won't / .
_____

5 When / soccer indoors / it rains / we usually play / .
_____

6 you go cycling / to wear a helmet / when / It is safer / .
_____

5 Complete the conversation with the missing words. (Circle) the correct options.

MARINA Do we ¹_____ go this way, Diego? Are you sure it's right?

DIEGO Yes, I'm sure. The map says if we ²_____ the path, we get to the hostel.

MARINA Did you check the route before we ³_____?

DIEGO Of course! But we ⁴_____ hurry. It's getting dark. Come on!

MARINA If I try to run, I ⁵_____ down. Ouch! Hey, Diego! Come back! Oh, no. My ankle!

DIEGO What's wrong? Why ⁶_____ there?

MARINA I ⁷_____ after you ⁸_____ I fell and sprained my ankle. It hurts!

DIEGO Oh, no! You should be more careful! Does it feel better if you ⁹_____ still? Or do you think you can walk on it?

MARINA Not sure. Is the hostel far from here?

DIEGO Well, I don't really know. Is your ankle still ¹⁰_____ it was?

MARINA Yes, it is. We could call for help. Does the phone work up here?

DIEGO No, sorry. Listen, you stay here, and I'll go for help. I ¹¹_____ long if I run. But you ¹²_____ move.

MARINA Don't worry, I can't! And please, hurry!

1 a must	b should	c have to
2 a follow	b will follow	c followed
3 a leave	b left	c were leaving
4 a must not	b shouldn't	c should
5 a won't fall	b 'll fall	c fell
6 a do you sit	b will you sit	c are you sitting
7 a ran	b was running	c 'm running
8 a when	b as	c while
9 a sat	b sit	c will sit
10 a as worse as	b worst	c as bad as
11 a won't be	b be	c 'm not
12 a must	b should	c must not

7 Are you connected?

VOCABULARY
Communication and Technology

1 ⭐ **Find ten more communication and technology words and phrases in the word snake.**

messageuploaddownloadappchipsocialmediadevicevideochatemojiscreensoftware

2 ⭐ **Circle the correct options.**

1 I usually send my mother a *device* / *message* if I'm not home on time.

2 When his dad's working in the U.S.A., Thomas often does a *video chat* / *social media* with him.

3 You can listen to music on your tablet or any other mobile *emoji* / *device*.

4 Our IT teacher wrote some *chips* / *software* for checking homework.

5 Blogs and other types of *social media* / *video chat* are a lot of fun.

6 Iris dropped her phone and broke the *app* / *screen* on it.

3 ⭐⭐ **Match the definitions with words from Exercise 1.**

1 copy information to a computer system or to the Internet. ___upload___

2 copy information onto a phone, tablet, laptop, etc. from the Internet or a computer. _____

3 the short word for an "application," for example, Spotify or Facebook. _____

4 a digital picture that shows a feeling or emotion. _____

5 a flat surface on a TV or computer where you can see words or pictures. _____

6 it's very small: the "brain" inside a computer or phone. _____

4 ⭐ **Match the words to make different collocations. Sometimes there is more than one possible answer.**

computer
~~download~~ social
electronic send
upload

media
devices
a message
~~software~~
screen
photos

download software, _____

_____

_____

5 ⭐⭐ **Complete the phone instructions with the correct form of words and phrases from Exercise 1.**

Thank you for buying a Techtime phone. When you turn on your new ¹___device___ for the first time, you will see an icon for "Games Shop" at the bottom of the ²_____. Here, you can ³_____ all your favorite social media, music, and news ⁴_____, like WhatsApp and Spotify. To write a ⁵_____ using text or email, press one of your contacts on the contacts list. The Techtime 1000 also has an excellent camera, so ⁶_____ with friends and family is easy!

Explore It! 🖱

True or false?

The average person checks their smartphone ten times a day.

Find another interesting fact about smartphones. Write a question and send it to a classmate in an email, or ask them in the next class.

READING
A Magazine Article

1 ⭐ **Look at the photo and the title of the article. What do you think the article is about? Read the article and check your ideas.** _____

High-Tech or No-Tech?

Juan Carlos García investigates how a school in California's Silicon Valley uses technology – or doesn't!

Silicon Valley in California has become the world center of technology, innovation, and social media. It's home to some of the world's biggest tech companies. So, with all this technology around, you probably think that all schools in Silicon Valley use lots of computers, laptops, and tablets in their classrooms, right? Wrong! In Masters Middle School, the school I visited, there isn't a tablet, screen, or smartphone anywhere. The classrooms have plants, traditional wooden desks, and even blackboards with colored chalks!

So why don't they use technology? The surprising thing is that the parents of these children – many of them technology experts at major tech companies – believe that bringing technology to class isn't a good idea! Many think that it doesn't help young people use their own minds. So, in this school, there are no electronic teaching devices in the classroom. Teachers here think that kids use their imaginations better without them!

This means that students don't use the Internet to study or upload apps to help them learn, and they use pens and paper to write, not tablets or laptops. They study their main subjects through artistic activities like music and painting. One student told me, "Our teachers believe that technology will only be helpful when we're older and we know how and when to use it properly."

So even the tech experts think that technology has its limits! High-tech or no-tech: which is the best? What do you think?

2 ⭐⭐ **Read the article again and check the meaning of these words in a dictionary. Then complete the sentences.**

> expert ~~imagination~~ innovation
> major minds properly

1 I'm not very good at writing stories because I have no _imagination_ .

2 My aunt knows a lot about computers. She's a technology _____ .

3 When you use this dictionary app _____, it's very easy to look up words.

4 This young company is famous for its _____ and new ideas.

5 My brother made a _____ decision to move to the U.S.A. to study.

6 People who develop software have creative _____ .

3 ⭐⭐ **Read the article again. Are the sentences *T* (true) or *F* (false)?**

1 Juan Carlos visited the school to learn about new classroom technology. _F_

2 The school is home to technology and innovation. ___

3 Juan Carlos expected to find a lot of electronic teaching devices in the school. ___

4 Some parents think that classroom technology stops young people from thinking creatively. ___

5 Students learn through artistic subjects. ___

6 Teachers believe that technology will never help students learn. ___

4 ⭐⭐⭐ **Answer the questions with your own ideas.**

1 How do some schools use technology in class?
_____

2 What electronic devices do you use in class to help you learn?
_____

GRAMMAR IN ACTION
Present Perfect: Affirmative and Negative

1 ⭐ **Complete the chart with the correct past participles.**

be	was	1 _____been_____
change	changed	2 _____
choose	chose	3 _____
do	did	4 _____
hear	heard	5 _____
learn	learned	6 _____
design	designed	7 _____
see	saw	8 _____

2 ⭐⭐ **Complete the sentences with the present perfect form of the verbs from Exercise 1.**

1 Kim ____has learned____ to use her new phone.

2 Technology _____ the way we learn.

3 YouTube _____ a popular video app for many years.

4 I _____ the new *Mission Impossible* movie. Don't miss it, it's great.

5 The students _____ their subjects for next year.

6 We _____ our math and IT homework.

7 I _____ a website for our basketball team.

8 Paul _____ the news, so you don't have to tell him.

3 ⭐ **Make the sentences negative.**

1 I've charged my phone.
   I haven't charged my phone.

2 Sergey's forgotten his password.
   _____

3 Wanda's broken her watch.
   _____

4 We've bought a new computer.
   _____

5 They've turned on the TV.
   _____

4 ⭐ **Write sentences with the present perfect.**

1 I / not finish / my homework for tomorrow
   I haven't finished my homework for tomorrow.

2 Alex / not read / anything about Silicon Valley
   _____

3 we / look for / some better information
   _____

4 they / buy / a new computer online
   _____

5 he / use / the latest software
   _____

6 the boys / not call / their parents
   _____

5 ⭐⭐ **Choose the correct verbs in each pair. Then complete the email with the present perfect form of the verbs.**

Dear Jess,

Good news! I ¹*'ve thrown* (throw / push) away my old tablet! Mom and Dad ² _____ (sell / buy) me a new laptop. I ³ _____ (upload / download) some great music software from the Internet, and I ⁴ _____ (decide / forget) to make a website for my band. I'm not sure if I told you, but I ⁵ _____ (stop / start) a band. Nick and I ⁶ _____ (write / listen) some music together. Nick ⁷ _____ (give / choose) the songs that we want to sing, but we still ⁸ _____ (not film / not record) anything.

More soon!

Theo

VOCABULARY AND LISTENING
Getting Around

1 ⭐ **Complete the transportation phrases with the missing vowels.**

1 g o o n f o o t
2 g _ t _ n _ tr _ _ n
3 g _ t _ ff _ b _ s
4 g _ t _ _ t _ f _ c _ r
5 g _ t _ nt _ _ t _ x _
6 g _ by tr _ m
7 t _ k _ _ pl _ n _

2 ⭐ **Match 1–6 with a–d.**

1 Our visitors got into ☐ d
2 We planned to catch ☐
3 I usually go by ☐
4 If you miss your bus, ☐
5 Which tram stop should I ☐
6 Is it better to cycle or go ☐

a bike when it isn't raining.
b you can catch the next one.
c on foot?
d their car and drove away.
e a plane from JFK Airport.
f get off at?

3 ⭐ **Circle the correct answers.**

1 I *get* / *go* by tram when I visit my friends in town.
2 Pete always goes to school *on* / *by* bike.
3 I get off the bus at this stop and go *by* / *on* foot from here.
4 My friend's *taken* / *gotten into* a plane to Peru.
5 Get *on* / *off* the train and find a seat by the window.
6 If you go *on* / *by* the subway, you get there quicker.
7 They can *catch* / *go by* a bus outside their house.
8 Marie got out *off* / *of* the car and hit her head on the door.

A Radio Interview

🎧 7.01 **4** ⭐ **Listen to the interview. Do Ellie and Joe think space tourism is just science fiction?**

_____

🎧 7.01 **5** ⭐⭐ **Listen again and circle the correct answers.**

1 The interview takes place ....
   a in a radio studio   c at a technology fair
   b at a school
2 Joe says he ... to drive.
   a loves   c doesn't need
   b hasn't learned
3 Ellie likes the idea of ....
   a driverless cars   b more bikes
   c faster bikes
4 She's seen an exhibit about ... in space.
   a movies   b astronauts   c travel
5 Joe thinks rockets to space will be ... today's jet planes.
   a the same as b different from c similar to
6 In Ellie's opinion, tourist trips to Mars in the next 20 years are ....
   a possible   b impossible   c a problem

6 ⭐⭐⭐ **Answer the questions.**

1 In your opinion, is a vacation on Mars just science fiction? Why / Why not?

_____

_____

2 If it becomes possible to go to space on vacation, do you think you will go? Why / Why not?

_____

_____

GRAMMAR IN ACTION
Will/Won't, May, and *Might*

1 ⭐ **Complete the sentences with *will* or *won't*.**

1 The photos you post online _____will_____ stay there for a long time.

2 Workers worry that robots _____ replace them and take their jobs.

3 I _____ work in another country in the future – I hate traveling.

4 Cars _____ need drivers in the future because of new driverless technology.

5 I think cities _____ become more bike friendly in future years because of all the traffic.

2 ⭐ (Circle) **the correct options.**

1 Maybe you should take a coat. It *will* / (*might*) be cold.

2 Smartphones will always be expensive. They *won't* / *might* get cheaper.

3 It's not certain, but we *will* / *may* go to school by helicopter in the future.

4 They *will* / *may* go by train, but they still haven't decided.

5 He *will* / *might* have his own bike one day – he's sure of that!

3 ⭐⭐ (Circle) **the correct options below to complete the email.**

● ● ●

TO: Josh	FROM: Lucy

Dear Josh,

I'm on a train with my mom and dad. They ¹_____ be away for the weekend, so I'm staying with my uncle Ted. It ²_____ be much fun there – it never is, 😟 but I'm sure I ³_____ chat with friends online. But then, who knows – there ⁴_____ be Wi-Fi in his house – I haven't asked! 😲 I'm sure he ⁵_____ have a TV, though – everyone has one! I ⁶_____ talk to you online this afternoon, but I don't know yet. Uncle Ted wants to go birdwatching! 😫

Lucy

1 (a) will   b won't   c might
2 a may not   b will   c won't
3 a may   b might   c will
4 a might not   b won't   c may
5 a won't   b will   c may
6 a may not   b will   c may

Infinitive of Purpose

4 ⭐⭐ **Rewrite the sentences with the infinitive of purpose.**

1 My sister and I went to New York. We wanted to visit the Transportation Museum.

   My sister and I went to New York to visit the Transportation Museum.

2 First, my sister went online. She checked the train times.

   _____

3 We walked to the station. We bought the tickets there.

   _____

4 I left the house at 6 a.m. I wanted to catch the first train.

   _____

5 My sister wanted to stop at a store. She needed to buy some sandwiches.

   _____

6 We got on the train quickly. That's how we got the best seats.

   _____

5 ⭐⭐ **Complete the text with the verbs and phrases in the box.**

may buy   might fly   to drive   ~~to get~~
to go   will travel

I normally use public transportation
¹____*to get*____ around. For example,
²_____ to school, I get the bus,
or I catch a tram. I ³_____ a
motorcycle when I'm old enough, or maybe
a car. I really don't know how my children
⁴_____ in the future. Maybe
they will have amazing machines
⁵_____ around in, or they
⁶_____ through the air.
Who knows?

WRITING
An Article

1 ⭐ **Read the article. Then circle the correct answer below.**

Technology has changed the way we … our friends.

a make contact with   c have fun with
b take care of

STAYING IN TOUCH: THEN AND NOW

① The way we communicate with our friends has changed a lot. ¹_____For_____ instance, when our grandparents were young, there were no cell phones, and what's ²_____, some families didn't even have a telephone at home. To call a friend, people needed to use a public phone.

② In contrast, today there are lots of ways of contacting friends. For ³_____, almost everyone can use a smartphone at any time and in any place. Posting status updates is easy with technology, such ⁴_____ online chats and messaging apps. In ⁵_____, we can send photos and videos to share special moments.

③ Some people think that friends might never meet face-to-face in the future. However, I don't think that will happen. It may become easier to "see" each other without actually meeting up, but it will always be more fun to sit and chat together.

2 ⭐⭐ **Complete the article with the words in the box.**

addition   as   example   ~~for~~   more

3 ⭐ **Read the article again and match 1–5 with a–e.**

1 In the past, there were   ☐ d
2 People needed to use a phone booth   ☐
3 Today we can use   ☐
4 It's easier now to share   ☐
5 It will always be more fun   ☐

a photos and videos with friends.
b smartphones to make calls at any time.
c to meet our friends face-to-face.
d no cell phones.
e to make contact with their friends.

4 ⭐ **Read the article again and write the correct paragraph number (1–3).**

a Which paragraph is about what might happen in the future?

_____

b Which paragraph mentions old technology? _____

c Which paragraph describes ways of communicating today?

_____

PLAN

5 ⭐⭐ **Write an article about doing homework. Think about homework in the past, present, and future. Take notes for each paragraph.**

1 How people did homework in the past:

_____

2 Technology for doing homework today:

_____

3 Predictions for the future:

_____

WRITE

6 ⭐⭐⭐ **Write your article. Remember to include past and present tenses, predictions with *will/won't* and *may/ might* (*not*), and phrases from the *Useful Language* box (see Student's Book, p89).**

CHECK

7 Do you …
• have three paragraphs?
• make certain and uncertain predictions for the future?

VOCABULARY

1 Put the letters in the correct order to make communication and technology words.

1 p a p _____
2 d v o i e t c a h _____
3 j i o m e _____
4 d o u l a p _____
5 l o i s c a d m i a e _____
6 w r o s t e f a _____
7 c r e n e s _____
8 p i h c _____
9 o w o d n l d a _____
10 v i e e d c _____
11 s g a e s e m _____

2 Look at the photos. What are the people doing? Complete the sentences with phrases for getting around.

GRAMMAR IN ACTION

3 Complete the conversation with the present perfect form of the verbs in parentheses.

DAD Jon, stop playing computer games now. It's time to eat.

JON I ¹_____ (not play) any games this evening, Dad! And I ²_____ (finish) my homework.

DAD Oh, OK. Well, that's good. I ³_____ (make) your favorite dinner.

JON Great, thanks. I ⁴_____ (send) Mom a message, but she ⁵_____ (not reply).

DAD Well, she ⁶_____ (fly) to Lisbon, so there's a time difference. I ⁷_____ (check) my emails, too, but I ⁸_____ (not hear) from her either. I'm sure she'll call us later.

1 Anna is _____*going on foot*_____.

2 Charlie is _____.

3 Helga is _____.

4 Kazuyo and Haru are _____.

5 David is _____.

6 Maria is _____.

4 Complete the dialogues with the infinitive of purpose or *will/won't*, *may*, or *might* (*not*). Use the verbs in the boxes. Sometimes there is more than one possible answer.

buy   not have   print

A Can I use your printer [1]_____ these photos, please?

B Not sure. I [2]_____ any paper. If there isn't enough, I think Dad [3]_____ some.

get   not take

A What time do we have to leave [4]_____ to the movie theater by six?

B There's no rush. We have time, and it [5]_____ long to get there.

be able to   play

A Do I need to download an app [6]_____ this game?

B You [7]_____ play it without one. Let's check!

be   edit

A What software does Sam use [8]_____ photos?

B I don't know, but he [9]_____ here in a minute, so you can ask him. OK?

CUMULATIVE GRAMMAR

5 Complete the conversation with the missing words. (Circle) the correct options.

CLAIRE Friday, at last! I'm happy it's over. I [1]_____ a tiring week. OK, see you later!

MARIK Hey, where [2]_____? Aren't you walking home?

CLAIRE No, I have a new bike. Didn't I tell you?

MARIK No, you [3]_____. When did you get that?

CLAIRE Last Saturday. It's great! It's the [4]_____ way to get around!

MARIK You [5]_____ really get a helmet, Claire! If you [6]_____, you'll hurt yourself.

CLAIRE I [7]_____ fall off, don't worry. I [8]_____ a helmet, but I just forgot it today.

MARIK Which one is your bike, then?

CLAIRE That blue one. It [9]_____ pretty cheap because I [10]_____ afford to spend much.

MARIK It's nice. You know, I [11]_____ get a bike. Then we can cycle to school together.

CLAIRE Good idea! But you'll need to ride fast [12]_____ with me! See you later!

1 a 've had   b was having   c 's had
2 a are you going   b do you go   c have you gone
3 a did   b not   c didn't
4 a best   b good   c better
5 a shouldn't   b may   c should
6 a fell off   b 'll fall off   c fall off
7 a don't   b won't   c must not
8 a bought   b 'm buying   c was buying
9 a were   b was being   c was
10 a couldn't   b can   c couldn't to
11 a might   b might not   c won't
12 a cycling   b to cycle   c for cycle

8 What is success?

VOCABULARY
Exceptional Jobs and Qualities

1 ⭐ **Complete the puzzle with words for jobs and qualities. Use the clues. What's the secret word in gray?**

1. He works for a company or organization, like a bank.
2. If you have this, you don't stop until you get what you want.
3. This person has ideas to make something completely new.
4. A runner, swimmer, high-jumper, etc.
5. This person designs and builds things.
6. This person writes music.
7. You need this to make something new and imaginative.
8. This person does experiments in a lab.
9. This person might produce books or songs.
10. With this, you can learn, understand, and form opinions.
11. You can do an activity or job well if you have this.
12. A natural ability to do something well.
13. You have this if you are strong, physically or mentally.

2 ⭐⭐ **Complete the sentences with words for qualities from Exercise 1.**

1. It takes a lot of ___skill___ to operate on a person's heart.
2. She won the prize for _____ for her original ideas. She has a great imagination.
3. Maya always shows great _____ and never stops trying to do her best.
4. The _____ of a chimpanzee is similar to a human's: chimpanzees are clever!
5. Hercules was famous for his _____. He could lift very heavy objects.

3 ⭐⭐ **Complete the sentences with words for jobs from Exercise 1 and the names in the box.**

> Adele   ~~Isaac Newton~~   Marie Curie
> Suzanne Collins   Tim Berners-Lee   Usain Bolt

1. _Isaac Newton_ was a _mathematician_ at Cambridge University in the 1600s.
2. The _____ of the World Wide Web is named _____.
3. _____ is the _____ of the song "Hello" from 2015.
4. _____ was a _____ who won two Nobel Prizes for important work on radioactivity.
5. _____ is a Jamaican _____ who was an Olympic champion in three different Olympic Games.
6. *The Hunger Games* series of novels is by a _____ named _____.

Explore It! 🖱️

Guess the correct answer.
Ashrita Furman has the world record for world records. He has over *100 / 200 / 300*.

Find another interesting fact about a world record. Write a question and send it to a classmate in an email, or ask them in the next class.

READING
Online Comments

1 ⭐ Read the online comments. Who has something in common with their hero? _____

<!-- browser window -->
● ● ●

| HOME | PROFILE | BLOG | PHOTOS |

FROM EARLY CHALLENGES TO ADULT SUCCESS!

Many of you liked our article last week about young adults who faced difficult times when they were kids but never stopped trying. Comments have flown in from all over the world!

An astrophysicist when he was still a teenager, Jake Barnett has made the biggest impression on me. Doctors said he had autism when he was two and that he might never speak. But he did, and he has shown an amazing talent for math. As an adult, Jake has an incredible memory and remembers every math problem he has ever solved!

Hooper 30 minutes ago

His name is Aaron "Wheelz" Fotheringham, and he's an amazing athlete. Now an adult, he needed a wheelchair when he was eight. He wanted to do tricks like his friends on skateboards and BMXs, so he took skateboard and BMX tricks and invented his own wheelchair tricks. You need strength and determination to become an extreme athlete when you can't use your legs. I use a wheelchair, and Aaron's had a big effect on me.

cre8tiv 35 minutes ago

Bethany Hamilton was 13 and already a great surfer when a shark attacked her and bit off her left arm. Three weeks after the accident, she got back into the water and continued surfing with only one arm! She wrote a book at 14, and a movie, *Soul Surfer*, followed. Now, as an adult, Bethany works hard helping others to face their challenges.

daisymay 45 minutes ago

2 ⭐⭐ Read the comments again and check the meaning of these words in a dictionary. Then complete the sentences.

> ~~autism~~   extreme   face
> tricks   wheelchair

1 A child with ___autism___ might not have good communication or social skills.

2 My brother used a _____ for a while after he broke both his legs.

3 We have to _____ our problems if we want to solve them.

4 Rock climbing is exciting and dangerous – it's one of the oldest _____ sports.

5 We've learned to do some great new _____ on our skateboards.

3 ⭐⭐ Read the comments again. Are the sentences *T* (true), *F* (false), or *DS* (doesn't say)?

1 Jake has an unusual talent for remembering numbers.   T

2 He's doing research in astrophysics. ___

3 Aaron invented new skateboard and BMX tricks. ___

4 A lot of people watch Aaron's wheelchair tricks online. ___

5 Bethany got back into the water three weeks after the shark attack. ___

6 First there was a movie about her, and after that she wrote a book. ___

4 ⭐⭐⭐ Answer the questions with your own ideas.

1 Which person in the comments has faced the biggest challenge? Why?

_____

2 Have you faced a big challenge? What was it?

_____

GRAMMAR IN ACTION
Present Perfect for Experience

1 ⭐ **Complete the sentences with the present perfect form of the verb in parentheses.**

1 I _'ve_ never _heard_ (hear) of Alexander Rybak.

2 A girl in my class _____ (win) a talent show.

3 Jess _____ (not be) to Spain.

4 They _____ (not see) *The Avengers*.

5 We _____ (raise) a lot of money for charity.

6 Max _____ (cycle) from Los Angeles to San Diego.

2 ⭐ **Match 1–6 with a–f.**

1 Have you ever drunk	[d]	a but only on YouTube.
2 Which European cities	[ ]	b to an email in English?
3 Our team has won	[ ]	c has she visited?
4 I've never read	[ ]	d carrot juice?
5 Have you ever replied	[ ]	e the book he gave me.
6 We've seen their band,	[ ]	f the championship three times.

3 ⭐⭐ **Write questions with the present perfect. Then look at the pictures to answer them.**

1 they / ever fly in a helicopter?

A _Have they ever flown in a helicopter?_

B _No, they haven't, but they've flown on a plane._

2 Fiona / ever sing in a band?

A _____

B _____

3 they / ever swim in the ocean?

A _____

B _____

4 your dad / ever make a cake?

A _____

B _____

4 ⭐⭐ **Underline and correct the mistake in each sentence.**

1 Have you ever <u>swim</u> with dolphins?
_____ swum _____

2 They never have been to the U.S.A.
_____

3 Never you have ridden a horse.
_____

4 Have she ever broken her phone?
_____

5 Stayed you ever in a five-star hotel?
_____

6 I'm happy to say I have ever lost my house keys. _____

5 ⭐⭐ **Complete the email with the present perfect form of the verbs and phrases in the box.**

> be   do   ~~fly~~   never explore
> never surf   ever try

Hi, Harry.
How are you? I'll be in Mexico in two weeks!
I ¹_'ve flown_ into Mexico City Airport before, but I ²_____ the country. My parents ³_____ on a lot of Mexican vacations, so they want to go to some new places. But they're also happy to revisit some of their favorite surfing beaches – they know I love the ocean! I ⁴_____, and I really want to learn. It can be dangerous, but I think I'll be OK! And ⁵_____ you _____ kite-surfing? My dad ⁶_____ it lots of times. I'm looking forward to watching him!
Bye for now!
Ava

VOCABULARY AND LISTENING
Phrasal Verbs: Achievement

1 ⭐ Match the phrasal verbs with the meanings.

1	work out	_e_
2	look up to	☐
3	give up	☐
4	set up	☐
5	come up with	☐
6	take part in	☐
7	show off	☐
8	keep up with	☐

a admire and respect someone

b act to attract attention, usually in a bad way

c start a new business

d join in an activity or event

e calculate something to get a result

f suggest or think of an idea or answer

g do what is necessary to stay equal or at the same level

h stop doing or having something

2 ⭐⭐ Complete the sentences with the correct form of phrasal verbs from Exercise 1. Then match them with photos (a–f).

1 Susie likes __working out__ hard math problems. _e_

2 It was so difficult that Hector decided to _____. __

3 Benjie _____ his dad and wants to be like him. __

4 Robin always _____ to the other band members. __

5 My little brother is a fast runner – no one can _____ him. __

6 Tanya really enjoyed _____ the race. __

a

b

c

d

e

f

A Talk

3 ⭐ Check the meaning of these words in a dictionary. Which words can you see in the photos?

> antibiotic   bacteria   mold
> Petri dish   reflect   shine

a

b

_____

_____

🎧 8.01 **4** ⭐ Listen to the talk. What do the two discoveries have in common?

_____

_____

🎧 8.01 **5** ⭐⭐ Listen again and (circle) the correct options.

1 The speaker describes the inventions as happy (accidents) / experiments.

2 The "cat's eyes" help drivers to see other drivers' lights / the middle of the road.

3 The inventor saw his car lights reflecting in a glass object / an animal's eyes.

4 Sir Alexander Fleming was studying bacteria / mold in a London hospital.

5 A person left the Petri dish open when Fleming was in hospital / on vacation.

6 Some mold was growing / killing the bacteria in the Petri dish.

6 ⭐⭐⭐ Choose one of the discoveries, cat's eyes or penicillin, and take notes for each heading in your notebook.

- name and nationality of the inventor

- country and place of discovery

- how the inventor discovered it

- why the discovery is important

GRAMMAR IN ACTION
Reflexive Pronouns

1 ⭐ Circle the correct options.

1 Peter is always looking at *himself* / *themselves* in the mirror!
2 You two should prepare *yourself* / *yourselves* for the test.
3 Have you ever taught *myself* / *yourself* a new skill?
4 The cat washes *yourself* / *itself* carefully every morning.
5 We embarrassed *ourselves* / *themselves* by showing off.
6 The girls entertained *themselves* / *herself* with video games.

2 ⭐⭐ Complete the sentences with reflexive pronouns and the correct form of the verbs in the box.

enter   imagine   make   ~~switch off~~   take care of   teach

1 The computer screen _switches itself off_ automatically.
2 Those kids are old enough to _____ .
3 Lauren and I _____ some new yoga exercises last week.
4 He _____ for three races in our sports event: running, cycling, and swimming.
5 Monica _____ a good lunch yesterday.
6 We often _____ as famous inventors.

Indefinite Pronouns

3 ⭐⭐ Put the words in the correct order to make sentences.

1 anyone / Mars / think / has / don't / walked / I / on
  I don't think anyone has walked on Mars.
2 phone / everywhere / her / She's / for / looked
  _____
3 will / tonight / Nobody / happen / what / knows
  _____
4 nowhere / on / to / bus / was / There / sit / the
  _____
5 new / broken / has / camera / Someone / my
  _____
6 do / help / Is / anything / I / there / can / to / ?
  _____

4 ⭐ Match 1–6 with a–f.

1 Has anyone seen ⬛ b
2 Mr. Kellogg invented ⬛
3 Everyone at the party ⬛
4 Olivia hasn't been ⬛
5 I get bored when ⬛
6 Everything was ready ⬛

a anywhere nice this summer.
b that documentary about inventors?
c I have nothing to do.
d when the first guests arrived.
e something by accident.
f had a great time.

5 ⭐⭐ Complete the text with the words in the box.

everyone   everywhere   himself
nobody   ~~someone~~   something
somewhere   themselves

Most of us admire [1] _someone_ who faces challenges and achieves great things. That's why [2] _____ I know looks up to the scientist Stephen Hawking. He lived [3] _____ near London until he went to Oxford University. There, he quickly proved [4] _____ to be a math genius. However, when he was only 21, doctors told him that he had [5] _____ called motor neurone disease (MND). [6] _____ usually lives long with MND, but Hawking didn't give up and, in fact, he lived another 55 years. When he couldn't walk, he used a wheelchair. Soon he lost his voice, so then he used a computerized voice to speak and write his books. He traveled [7] _____ , giving talks and showing the world what people can achieve when they believe in [8] _____ .

WRITING
A Competition Entry

1 ⭐ **Read the advertisement. What do you have to do to enter the competition?**

_____

> ### YOUNG HEROES CLUB ANNUAL COMPETITION
>
> Send us your entry! Describe how you have helped someone who has faced a challenge. Tell us:
> - the greatest help you have given someone
> - how you did it
> - what advice you have for other young helpers
>
> The best entry will receive a special award from a mystery celebrity!

2 ⭐ **Read the competition entry. What has Gabriela's brother achieved?**

_____

My name is Gabriela. My brother Jamie has learning difficulties, and he has faced many challenges.

One of Jamie's ¹_____ is learning to make friends. He can't speak clearly, and because of this it's sometimes difficult for him to make new friends. At first, he was very shy, so I decided to help him. However, after ²_____, I've managed to bring a group of friends into Jamie's life.

How ³_____ it? First of all, I asked our parents to get Jamie a drum. He has always loved music, so he loved the drum! One day, I invited some musician friends to our house. They introduced themselves to Jamie and then just played some music. Soon Jamie started to play with them. Two of these friends have now formed a band, and Jamie is their drummer.

If you want to help someone make friends, my ⁴_____ is to find something they love doing and help them meet people with the same interest. And never give up!

3 ⭐ **Complete the competition entry with the phrases in the box.**

> a lot of effort   advice to you
> did I do   greatest achievements

4 ⭐⭐ **Read the competition entry again and answer the questions.**

1 What challenge does Jamie face?

_____

2 Why did his sister decide to help him?

_____

3 What did Jamie's parents buy him?

_____

4 How many people are in Jamie's band?

_____

PLAN

5 ⭐⭐ **Write a competition entry. Take notes about how you helped a person for the competition in Exercise 1.**

1 Introduce yourself and the person you helped: _____

2 Explain what you did: _____

3 Explain how you did it: _____

4 Give advice for other people: _____

WRITE

6 ⭐⭐⭐ **Write your competition entry. Remember to include the present perfect, reflexive pronouns, vocabulary from this unit, and phrases from the _Useful Language_ box (see Student's Book, p101).**

CHECK

7 **Do you …**
- have four paragraphs?
- explain your achievement clearly?
- give useful advice?

VOCABULARY

1 Look at the pictures and (circle) the correct options.

1 *athlete / engineer*   2 *inventor / composer*   3 *engineer / writer*   4 *businesswoman / mathematician*

5 *athlete / scientist*   6 *composer / writer*   7 *mathematician / writer*   8 *businesswoman / athlete*

2 Put the letters in **bold** in the correct order to make words for qualities.

1 She admired the **vaiittcyre** of the architect who designed her new home. _____

2 Carlos Acosta showed great **letant** as a dancer from an early age. _____

3 Rock climbers need physical **gshtnert**.

_____

4 Her **eignelelictn** was clear from the clever answers she gave. _____

5 His **ndoeittearnmi** to win made him practice for hours. _____

3 (Circle) the correct options.

1 My sister finishes her homework so fast. It's hard to *keep up / come up* with her.

2 We all *look up to / keep up with* our teachers and listen to their advice.

3 If you want to *show off / take part in* the competition, fill out this entry form.

4 Can you help me *give up / work out* this problem?

5 Let's *give up / set up* a volunteer organization to help our community.

6 If I don't *come up with / keep up with* a good idea soon, I'll *show off / give up*.

GRAMMAR IN ACTION

4 Complete the sentences with the present perfect form of the verbs in the box.

> be   break   hear   read   see

1 _____ you ever _____ of a mathematician named Maryam Mirzakhani?

2 I _____ never _____ a book about astrophysics.

3 He _____ never _____ a world record, but I'm sure he will one day.

4 _____ Philip ever _____ a Studio Ghibli movie?

5 _____ we _____ here before? I don't remember it.

5 Correct the <u>underlined</u> reflexive and indefinite pronouns.

1 My cat has taught <u>myself</u> to open the fridge door. _____

2 Mrs. Howe is <u>nobody</u> who I've always looked up to. _____

3 Mary Ann saw <u>themselves</u> in a video clip on YouTube. _____

4 We've looked <u>anywhere</u> for our lost door keys. _____

5 You often talk to <u>ourselves</u> when you're alone. I've heard you! _____

6 I think there's <u>anything</u> wrong with my computer. _____

7 I've noticed that my brother looks at <u>herself</u> in the mirror a lot. _____

8 There was <u>anybody</u> in the house; it was empty. _____

CUMULATIVE GRAMMAR

6 Complete the conversation with the missing words. (Circle) the correct options.

JILL   Oh, no. I ¹_____ to write a 500-word essay for Mr. Jenkins.

PETE   Uh, and you've come to me ²_____ some ideas, right?

JILL   Yes, please! The title is "³_____ Creative Person I Know".

PETE   Can't you think of ⁴_____?

JILL   Well, ⁵_____ my aunt Louella?

PETE   I think I saw her once when she ⁶_____ with you.

JILL   Maybe. She ⁷_____ us very often, but it's possible.

PETE   I'll probably remember her if you ⁸_____ her.

JILL   She's my mom's sister. She's ⁹_____ tall as Mom, but she's slim and blond. Anyway, I look up to her because she's achieved a lot, and she hasn't had ¹⁰_____ easy life.

PETE   Really?

JILL   Well, no. She was often sick as a teenager, and she didn't go to college, but she taught ¹¹_____ to paint. Now she has exhibitions ¹²_____.

PETE   So, I think you have your topic, Jill, without any help from me!

1 a	must	b have	c don't have
2 a	getting	b and get	c to get
3 a	The Most	b Most	c The More
4 a	nobody	b anybody	c nothing
5 a	have you met ever	b have you ever met	c did you ever met
6 a	is staying	b stays	c was staying
7 a	doesn't visit	b don't visit	c isn't visiting
8 a	may describe	b describe	c will describe
9 a	not as	b more	c not the
10 a	some	b any	c an
11 a	herself	b her	c himself
12 a	nowhere	b everywhere	c somewhere

VOCABULARY
Musical Instruments and Genres

1 ⭐ Put the letters in the correct order to make musical instruments and genres. Then complete the chart with the words.

> ~~honroicpem~~   ~~garege~~   olivin   ssab   lkfo
> ssiclacal   ugarit   orkc   phaxosone   rumsd
> phi-oph   rpumtet   bekyarod   azjz

Instruments	Genres
microphone	reggae

2 ⭐⭐ Look at the band members (1–8) in the picture and complete the text with words from Exercise 1.

HOME   ABOUT ME   ARCHIVE   FOLLOW

There are eight of us in our band. Bruno plays the ¹_drums_. We have Janina on ²_____, and her brother Stefan plays the ³_____. Rob plays the ⁴_____, and he's really good! Sally's just started to play the ⁵_____, but we love her, and she's learning fast. Simon's a classical musician, but he plays an electric ⁶_____ with us. He's really talented. Ramon plays the ⁷_____, and that's Katie at the front. She's our singer, of course, and she doesn't really need that ⁸_____ – she has a great voice!

3 ⭐⭐ Match the photos with the musical genre words from Exercise 1.

1 _____rock_____   2 _____

3 _____   4 _____

5 _____   6 _____

4 ⭐⭐ Which word in each group does not follow the same stress pattern?

1 (●)   folk   bass   reggae   drums
2 (●•)   reggae   guitar   trumpet   keyboard
3 (●••) violin   classical microphone saxophone

5 ⭐⭐⭐ Think of an example of a song or piece of music for each musical genre from Exercise 1. Use the Internet to help you if necessary.

_____
_____
_____

Explore It! 🖱

Guess the correct answer.

The world's longest officially released song is *The Rise and Fall of Bossanova*. It is about 3 / 13 / 23 hours long.

Find another interesting fact about a song. Write a question and send it to a classmate in an email, or ask them in the next class.

READING
An Events Guide

1 ⭐ **Read the events guide. Do you think this is a good school party? Why / Why not?**

2 ⭐⭐ **Read the events guide again and check the meaning of these words in a dictionary. Then complete the sentences.**

> available ~~joke~~ latest mix provide set

1 I never know if Juan's being serious or telling a _____joke_____.
2 The band began their _____ at eight and finished playing at nine.
3 We will _____ all the information you need for your trip.
4 Tickets for next week's concerts are now _____ online.
5 I think the _____ hit from Catfish is the best song they've ever written.
6 Tina's music is a _____ of hip-hop and reggae.

3 ⭐⭐ **Read the events guide again. Answer the questions.**

1 How much are tickets if you buy them before you go to the party?

_____

2 Is the party indoors or outdoors?

_____

3 What can the students drink?

_____

4 What can the students do in the last 30 minutes of DJ Quin's set?

_____

5 Why will people be surprised by the special guest?

_____

6 What is special about the band Born to Be Wild?

_____

4 ⭐⭐⭐ **Answer the questions with your own ideas.**

1 In your opinion, which performer at the party will be the best?

_____

2 Have you ever had an end-of-year party at school? What was it like?

_____

GRAMMAR IN ACTION

Going To

1 ⭐ **Write sentences with *going to*.**

1 I / take some photos

I'm going to take some photos.

2 She / watch TV

_____

3 He / not answer the phone

_____

4 Faye / play the piano

_____

5 They / record a song

_____

2 ⭐⭐ **Complete the sentences with *going to* and the verbs in the box.**

> be   bring   not tell   ~~organize~~   see

1 I 'm going to organize a party for my best friend.

2 We _____ her anything about it.

3 Carmen _____ food and drinks to the party.

4 We _____ a folk-rock concert.

5 The party _____ in my garage.

3 ⭐⭐ **Write sentences about the people with *going to* and the phrases in the box.**

> enter a talent competition   ~~get a job as a DJ~~
> get free concert tickets   run a marathon   study singing

1 Nasrin loves making playlists and discovering new music.

Nasrin's going to get a job as a DJ.

2 I've always wanted to go to music college.

_____

3 Lily dreams of becoming a comedian.

_____

4 Finn and Livvy run and train hard every day.

_____

5 Max and I are lucky: we have a friend in the band.

_____

Will and Going To

4 ⭐ **Complete the sentences with *will* or *won't*.**

1 He's sure it _____will_____ be a great event because the guide looked interesting.

2 I _____ pay $150 for a ticket – that's too much.

3 Your parents _____ get angry if your music is too loud, so turn it down.

4 _____ all three sisters sing in the same band?

5 It _____ be cold at the party, so you don't need a coat.

5 ⭐⭐ **Decide if the sentences are predictions or intentions. Then (circle) the best options to complete the conversations.**

1 A What *(are you going to)* / *will you* do this evening?

B I'm going to / 'll see a show at the City Hall.

2 A What *are you going to* / *will you* sing? Have you decided?

B No, but I promise you *'ll* / *'re going to* like it!

3 A I'm going to / will learn the saxophone.

B You*'ll* / *'re going to* be good at that. I just know it!

4 A The Headsets *aren't going to* / *won't* tour anymore.

B Oh, no. That *won't* / *isn't going to* be very popular with their fans.

6 ⭐⭐ **Complete the chat with the correct form of *will* or *going to* and the verbs in parentheses.**

¹ _____Are_____ you _going to be_ (be) at home later?

No, I ² _____ (meet) my dad at the music store. I've decided: I ³ _____ (ask) him to buy me that guitar I saw in the window.

Really? You know you ⁴ _____ (get) a better price online.

Yeah, but I ⁵ _____ (try) it before we buy it – that's my plan anyway.

Well, OK, but do you play the guitar?

No, I don't, but I'm sure I ⁶ _____ (learn) fast! It can't be that difficult.

VOCABULARY AND LISTENING

Dance Styles

A Discussion

1 ⭐ **Match five of the dance styles in the box with the shoes the dancers wear.**

> ~~ballet dancing~~   ballroom dancing   breakdancing
> folk dance   disco dancing   modern dance
> salsa dancing   swing   tap dancing   Zumba

1 _ballet dancing_

2 _____

3 _____

4 _____

5 _____

2 ⭐ (Circle) **the correct options.**

1 In the 1970s, (disco) / *ballet* dancing was a popular dance in nightclubs.

2 *Salsa / Tap* dancing is a type of dance from Latin America.

3 *Breakdancing / Swing* is a strong, exciting style of jazz dancing with a partner.

4 My grandparents don't like *modern / folk* dance. They prefer more traditional performances.

5 *Swing / Zumba* is a type of exercise, often in a class, with dance movements.

🎧 9.01 **3** ⭐⭐ **Listen to the discussion and answer the questions.**

1 How many speakers do you hear? _____

2 How many are male and how many are female?

_____

_____

🎧 9.01 **4** ⭐⭐ **Listen again. Are the sentences *T* (true) or *F* (false)?**

1 The class is going to report back on their discussion next week. _F_

2 The after-school classes start next week. ___

3 One of the teachers is planning a school talent show. ___

4 Jessica wants to do modern dance. ___

5 Camila wants to do sports next semester. ___

6 Enzo wants to have a PE class after school. ___

5 ⭐⭐⭐ **Answer the questions.**

1 What music or dance activities can you do at your school?

_____

2 What other after-school activities or clubs does your school have?

_____

GRAMMAR IN ACTION
Present Continuous for Future

1 ⭐ **Complete the sentences with the present continuous form of the verbs in parentheses.**

1 Our school _'s performing_ (perform) a musical next term.

2 Katie _____ (help) with the costumes after school.

3 Ms. Wilson _____ (teach) us the dance moves next week.

4 Who _____ (write) the programs for the new musical?

5 I _____ (not play) in the orchestra next time.

6 _____ you _____ (come) to watch the show tonight?

2 ⭐ **Write sentences with the present continuous.**

1 the musicians / leave for New York tomorrow

The musicians are leaving for New York tomorrow.

2 they / perform three evening concerts in July

_____

3 a journalist / interview the lead singer later

_____

4 a TV camera operator / record tomorrow's show

_____

5 the drummer / not play with the band tonight

_____

6 he / fly to New York next week to study music there

_____

3 ⭐⭐ **Complete the sentences with the present continuous form of the verbs in the box.**

arrive   cook   ~~help~~   not come   not do   watch

1 Jonny _is helping_ his sister with her homework later.

2 The boys _____ a movie after school.

3 I _____ pasta tonight. Who wants to come?

4 Helena's busy, so she _____ to the theater with us.

5 When _____ the stars of the show _____?

6 We _____ anything special tonight.

Simple Present for Future

4 ⭐ **Complete the sentences with the simple present form of the verbs in parentheses.**

1 The next show ___starts___ (start) at eight.

2 The singers _____ (arrive) at five in the afternoon.

3 Our train _____ (leave) at six the next morning.

4 Tomorrow's rehearsal _____ (not end) until the evening.

5 ⭐⭐ **Write questions for the answers from Exercise 4.**

1 What time _does the next show start_ ?

2 When _____ ?

3 What time _____ ?

4 When _____ ?

6 ⭐⭐ (Circle) **the correct options.**

ADAM	¹(Are you doing) / Do you do anything this afternoon?
AVA	Yes, my big brother and I ²meet / are meeting our cousin Greg outside the club. He ³'s coming / comes to stay with us after his performance.
ADAM	Oh, yes – the rapper! ⁴Don't you watch / Aren't you watching his show?
AVA	I've seen it twice! We ⁵'re getting / get something to eat on the way home.
ADAM	What time ⁶is the show ending / does the show end?
AVA	It ⁷ends / 's ending at 7:30, so we ⁸'re going / go to that new Italian place. We ⁹buy / 're buying pizza to take home for dinner!

WRITING
A Review

1 ⭐ **Read the review. Where is the performance taking place?** _____

Twelve – the Musical! ★★★★★

This year's 12th grade students have formed a unique song and dance group. Their show, called *Twelve – the Musical!*, tells the story of Kurt Goldberg, a theater director, and the dancers who want to perform in his show. The music is a mix of disco and swing. Some of 12th grade's best musicians also play their own songs.

It's a classic story of dancers who come to the city to become famous. I was <u>very impressed</u> by the beautiful costumes and creative makeup, and Chris Randall is superb as Kurt Goldberg. However, the <u>highlight</u> of the show was the singing. Chris has a powerful voice, and the dancers' songs were often funny. On the <u>downside</u>, the set was not very exciting.

Twelve – the Musical! is on again in the auditorium next Friday and Saturday. After graduating, Chris is leaving to study opera, and others in the group are continuing their theater studies at different colleges in the U.S.A. <u>All in all</u>, <u>if you love</u> music, this unique musical is <u>a must-see</u>.

2 ⭐ **Complete the sentences with the <u>underlined</u> phrases in the review.**

1 I was <u>very impressed</u> by the funny script.

2 So, _____ hip-hop, this show is for you.

3 The _____ of the show was the superb tap dancing. I loved it!

4 For anyone who enjoys jazz, this show is _____.

5 On the _____, the lead guitarist didn't play well.

6 _____, it's a show you mustn't miss.

3 ⭐⭐ **Which things do these adjectives describe?**

1 unique — *the song and dance group*

2 classic — _____

3 beautiful — _____

4 creative — _____

5 superb — _____

6 powerful — _____

7 funny — _____

8 not exciting — _____

PLAN

4 ⭐⭐ **Write a review of a school show that you have seen or been in. Take notes about these things.**

1 A general description of the show:

_____

2 Details about the dancing, music, costumes, etc., and what you liked / didn't like:

_____

3 A summary of your opinion:

_____

WRITE

5 ⭐⭐⭐ **Write your review. Remember to use adjectives, the simple present to describe the show, the simple past for your opinion, and phrases from the *Useful Language* box (see Student's Book, p113).**

CHECK

6 Do you ...

- use three paragraphs?
- say what you liked and didn't like?
- summarize your opinions at the end?

VOCABULARY

1 Look at the photos and complete the descriptions below with words for musical instruments and genres.

1 Katrina plays the _____ . She has studied _____ music.

2 Bryony loves _____ music and plays the _____ in the park.

3 Marius is a great _____ artist. All he needs is his _____ to speak into.

4 Monica plays the _____ in a reggae band, and Milton plays the _____ .

5 Ella plays the _____ , and Joe plays the _____ in their band.

6 Our music teacher plays the _____ at a _____ club.

2 Find ten dance styles in the wordsnake.

discosalsatapballroombreakdancingZumbaswingfolkballetmodern

GRAMMAR IN ACTION

3 Complete the email with the correct form of *going to* or *will* and the verbs in the box.

be   bring   cost   finish   go
have   meet   not rain

TO: Jed

FROM: Liam

Dear Jed,

Aidan and I ¹_____ to a music festival on the weekend. Do you remember Jake and Ida? They ²_____ us there. I ³_____ all my homework first so I can really relax and enjoy myself! Aidan ⁴_____ sandwiches and hot drinks because we think the festival food ⁵_____ a lot – it's always expensive! I hope it ⁶_____ on Friday, but I bet it ⁷_____ cloudy all weekend. I'm not worried about that – I'm sure we ⁸_____ fun.

Hope your weekend's fun, too!

See you soon,
Liam

4 (Circle) the correct options.

1 I'*m not doing* / *don't do* anything special this afternoon.

2 The program says the music *starts* / *is starting* at 8:30 p.m.

3 People *are arriving* / *arrive* at seven tonight for the party.

4 *Are you using* / *Do you use* that microphone tonight?

5 Who'*s writing* / *writes* the songs for next year's show?

6 The ticket office *opens* / *is opening* tomorrow at 9 a.m.

7 A really exciting event *is happening* / *happens* at our school next week.

8 You'll have to run for the last bus because the show *isn't ending* / *doesn't end* until 10:30.

CUMULATIVE GRAMMAR

5 Complete the conversation with the missing words. (Circle) the correct options.

HARRY Have you ¹_____ of SoGood Sounds?

TINA If they ²_____ a reggae band, I won't know them. I don't know as much about that kind of music ³_____ you do.

HARRY No, no, there's an organization called SoGood Sounds. ⁴_____ of them?

TINA No. What ⁵_____?

HARRY They organize outdoor music festivals ⁶_____ money for charities. They're all musicians, and they raise money for disabled people because some of them need assistance to take care of ⁷_____.

TINA Oh, I see. Do you know ⁸_____ more about the music they play?

HARRY Not really. I think that there ⁹_____ be one of their concerts next weekend, but I'm not sure. I ¹⁰_____ to look on the website tonight.

TINA OK, so when you get ¹¹_____ information, can you text me?

HARRY Of course. I'll do that if I ¹²_____, no problem!

1 a heard ever	b ever heard	c ever hear
2 a are	b will be	c won't be
3 a like	b than	c as
4 a Did you hear	b Have you heard	c Were you hearing
5 a they do	b are they doing	c do they do
6 a to raise	b for raise	c for raising
7 a itself	b themselves	c theirselves
8 a anything	b anywhere	c anyone
9 a has to	b might	c might to
10 a will	b 'm going	c should
11 a an	b a	c some
12 a 'm remembering	b 'll remember	c remember

EXAM TIPS: Reading Skills

Reading: Multiple Choice

You will read a long text, which is often based on a newspaper or magazine article. This tests your understanding of the most important ideas and some details of the text. The title tells you what the topic is. There are multiple-choice questions. To answer the questions, you need to choose the correct answer, A, B, or C.

Example:

How does Estefania feel about the school exchange trip?

A She's excited to meet new people.

B She's worried about speaking a new language.

C She's nervous about being away from home for the first time.

Exam Guide: Multiple Choice

- Start by reading the title of the text so you know what the topic is.

- Read the whole text quickly first to find out more about the topic and to get a general understanding.

- Read the text again more carefully to get a better understanding. Use the context to work out the meaning of any new vocabulary, but don't spend too much time worrying about unfamiliar words at this point.

- Now read all the questions carefully and <u>underline</u> the important "key" words in the questions. This helps you when you look for the same information in the text.

  Example:

  How does <u>Estefania</u> <u>feel</u> about the <u>school</u> <u>exchange</u> <u>trip</u>?

- Read the first question again. Then look for the part of the text where you think you might find the answer. If you remember something from when you read through the text, go back to that part first to check. If not, read from the beginning until you find what you need.

- When you find the relevant part of the text, <u>underline</u> the words and write the number of the question next to the words you underlined. Then circle the option in the question, A, B, or C, that most closely matches the meaning in the text. Use the key words in the question to help you.

  Example:

  <u>*I'm really happy to go to Chicago to learn English and stay with an English-speaking family, and I don't mind being away from home, but I hope I won't forget the English I already know and I can understand everyone!*</u>

- Remember to check the other two options as well to decide why they aren't correct.

- Now read the other questions and repeat the process until you finish.

> ### REMEMBER!
>
> The text often mentions information from all three options in the question, but only one option is correct. Read the text carefully and match the meaning, not the words.

Reading Practice: Multiple Choice

1 <u>Underline</u> the key words in the questions.

1 *<u>What</u> <u>after-school</u> <u>activities</u> does <u>Lena</u> <u>like</u> <u>doing</u> on <u>Mondays</u>?*

2 What day does Tom prefer playing tennis with his brother?

3 Why does Mason think art classes are difficult?

4 Who prefers studying alone to studying with other people?

5 How did Eva feel on the morning of her exam?

6 What, according to Josh, is the best thing about eating lunch at home?

> **Tip!**
> "Key" words carry the meaning in a sentence: they are usually nouns, adjectives, verbs, adverbs, and question words. Underlining these words in questions can help you to focus on the information you need to find in the text.

2 <u>Underline</u> the key words in questions 1–5. Then match 1–5 with A–E.

1 What's Ben doing with his friends now? ☐

2 What did Ben do last weekend with his aunt? ☐

3 Where did Ben arrange to see his friend last week? ☐

4 What does Ben do Monday to Friday after school? ☐

5 Where does Ben go on Saturdays? ☐

A He met him in the park on Friday.

B He plays basketball during the week.

C Today, they're at the gym.

D He goes to computer club every weekend.

E On Saturday, he went to the movies with her.

3 Choose the option, A, B, or C, which has the same meaning as each sentence (1–3). Then <u>underline</u> the words and phrases which helped you to match the sentences.

> **Tip!**
> Look out for words or phrases which look different in the questions and text but have the same meaning; for example, synonyms, or antonyms with a negative verb.

1 *Lily <u>hates</u> going to her grandma's after school.*

Ⓐ Lily <u>really doesn't like</u> going to her grandma's after school.

B Lily doesn't mind going to her grandma's after school.

C Lily likes going to her grandma's after school.

2 Harry was nervous about the exam scores.

A Harry wasn't worried about the exam scores.

B Harry felt worried about the exam scores.

C Harry was excited about the exam scores.

3 We were tired after the trip.

A We didn't have much energy after the trip.

B The trip was tiring, but we felt OK after it.

C We were full of energy after the trip.

4 My parents are upset with me.

A My parents aren't unhappy with me.

B My parents aren't angry with me.

C My parents aren't very happy with me.

4 Read the text and match the words in **bold** with the synonyms 1–5.

Last night our neighbors were on a game **show** on TV! Mr. and Mrs. Jackson seemed pretty **worried** at the beginning of the show because they were losing. Mr. Jackson looked **scared** and couldn't answer his questions very well, but Mrs. Jackson answered her questions **with no difficulty**. The final question was for the Jackson team, and they thought about it **with care** before answering. They got the answer **right** and won the game in the end, which was fantastic!

1 nervous _____ worried _____

2 easily _____

3 carefully _____

4 program _____

5 correct _____

6 afraid _____

EXAM TIPS: Reading Skills

Reading: Open Cloze

You will fill in blanks in a short, simple text using one word only per blank. All words must be spelled correctly. This tests your knowledge of parts of speech such as verbs, determiners, prepositions, and pronouns. There is one example in the text, marked "0."

Example:

Have you (0) _____ the new Fantastic Beasts *movie?*

Exam Guide: Open Cloze

- First, read the text quickly to find out the topic and understand the general meaning.

- Think about the possible words that might go in the blanks as you read through.

- Look carefully at the words before and after each blank, and read the whole sentence before deciding on an appropriate answer. Underline any important words.

- If you are not sure of an answer, move to the next item. You can do the ones you find easiest first and come back to the more difficult ones at the end.

- For difficult items, use the words before and after the blank to try to figure out the part of speech. For example, if the blank is preceded by a subject pronoun, the missing word is probably a verb. If it comes after a verb or a noun, it may be a preposition.

- If you think that more than one answer is possible, think very carefully about the sentence and the structure again. Read the sentence over in your head with both alternatives. Choose the word you feel fits best. Sometimes there is more than one possible answer, but remember you can write only ONE of these correct words in the blank.

  Example:

  *Have you **seen** the new* Fantastic Beasts *movie yet?*

  *Have you **watched** the new* Fantastic Beasts *movie yet?*

- When you have fill in all the blanks, read the whole text again carefully to check your answers and spelling.

> **REMEMBER!**
>
> The most common parts of speech are pronouns (e.g., *her*), determiners (e.g., *some*), conjunctions (e.g., *because*), time expressions (e.g., *since*), auxiliary verbs (e.g., *would*), and prepositions (e.g., *in*).

Reading Practice: Open Cloze

Tip! Look at the words before and after the blank to decide what part of speech the missing word is.

1 What type of word is missing in each sentence? Choose the correct parts of speech.

1 *We saw* _____ *great movie last night.* <u>article</u> / *verb*

2 *Noel fell* _____ *his skateboard and hurt his knee.* *preposition / verb*

3 *He bought* _____ *girlfriend a new pair of shoes.* *preposition / possessive adjective*

4 *You don't* _____ *to come if you don't want to.* *verb / determiner*

5 *She's put too* _____ *salt in the food.* *determiner / conjunction*

6 _____ *does Lisa live?* *time expression / question word*

7 *Let's buy Lucy a present* _____ *it's her birthday.* *conjunction / pronoun*

2 Complete the sentences in Exercise 1 with the correct missing words.

3 Read the text and correct the words in bold.

Tip! Remember to read the whole text again when you finish. Check that you have used the correct verb forms, e.g., *She* ~~have~~ **has** *never been to Boston.*

⁰**Does** you know Corey's cousin, James? He's ¹**a** athlete! He ²**win** two gold medals for ³**her** school last year, and he wants to ⁴**running** in the county championships next month. He exercises five times a week ⁵**on** the gym, and he always tries to do ⁶**best** each time. He's ⁷**so** talented as the other athletes, and I believe he can win the championships ⁸**on** the future.

1 _Do_   3 _____   5 _____   7 _____   9 _____

2 _____   4 _____   6 _____   8 _____

4 Choose the correct missing words to complete the sentences.

1 *… it rain last night?*   *a Has*   ⓑ *Did*   *c Was*

2 I can't do this question. It's … hard!   a too   b enough   c as

3 Kerry did very … on the exams.   a good   b bad   c well

4 The alarm went off … our math class.   a at   b during   c while

5 You … run in the school hallways.   a don't   b must   c shouldn't

6 Were you … to call me just now?   a trying   b tried   c try

5 Match one word from each box with each blank.

| can ~~if~~ need on very what |

| could have off really ~~when~~ which |

Tip! Sometimes more than one word can be used to fill in a blank – though this isn't very common. When you think there is more than one possibility, write only one in the blank. Try to choose the option which you think is the most common.

1 *… you heat ice, it melts.*   _If_ _When_

2 I thought I did badly on the test, but I got a … good score!   _____ _____

3 … country did you go to on vacation?   _____ _____

4 We … to get to the station by ten o'clock to catch the train.   _____ _____

5 … you open the window, please?   _____ _____

6 Do you know how to turn … this computer?   _____ _____

EXAM TIPS: Listening Skills

Listening: Matching

You will listen to a conversation between two people who know each other and match information in two lists of items. You will hear the conversation twice. This tests your understanding of detailed information. Before you listen to the conversation, you will hear instructions explaining who is speaking and what they are talking about.

Example:

*You will hear **Josh and Stella** talking about **the band for a new school musical**.*

You need to match the items in the first list with the correct items in the second list. There are five items in the first list and eight in the second: there are three extra items you don't need.

Example:

You will hear Josh and Stella talking about the band for a new school musical. Which musical instrument is each person going to play?

1	Josh	A	keyboard
2	Stella	B	drums
3	Kristie	C	guitar
4	Ella	D	piano
5	Adam	E	trumpet
		F	violin
		G	bass guitar
		H	saxophone

Exam Guide: Matching

- You will have time before you listen to read the question and look at the lists. Read them carefully and think about the context so you know what you can expect to hear.

- You will see that all the words in each list belong to the same vocabulary group. The first list is usually people and the second list is a group of nouns such as sports, food, or musical instruments. In the recording, you will hear the items in the first list in the same order in which they appear on the page.

- When you listen the first time, try to understand the general meaning of the conversation and think about the best option for each answer. If you aren't sure, don't worry. The second time you listen, you can check your first answer or make another choice.

- The first time you listen, you can also try to identify the items in the second list that are not needed. You can then cross these out so you can focus only on the other items when you listen the second time.

- When you listen the second time, focus more on specific information and check your answers carefully.

REMEMBER!

It's important to know when to stop focusing on a question you're not sure about so that you don't miss the next question. Don't spend too long on one item – try and follow the conversation. You can revise your answers when you listen the second time or at the end.

Listening Practice: Matching

🎧 **1** Read the instruction and question, and answer the
E.01   questions below. Then listen and check your ideas.

**You will hear Josh and Stella talking about the band
for a new school musical. Which musical instrument is
each person going to play?**

> **Tip!**
> Always read the instructions and
> question carefully before you listen to
> the conversation. This will help you to
> think about the context and anticipate
> what you are going to hear.

1 Why do you think they're talking about the band for the school musical?

_____

2 What kinds of words do you think you will hear in the conversation?

_____

3 Where do you think they are having their conversation?

_____

🎧 **2** Listen to the conversations.
E.02   **Which item is mentioned but
isn't the correct answer in each
conversation? Put a cross (✗)
next to the incorrect options.**

> **Tip!**
> When you listen, you may hear an item from the second list
> mentioned in the conversation that isn't necessarily the correct answer.
> Listen carefully and try to eliminate items which aren't the correct option.

1 Sally enjoys watching …   a comedies. ☐   b dramas. ☒   c soap operas. ☐

2 For the picnic, Joe needs to bring …   a a cake. ☐   b fruit. ☐   c sandwiches. ☐

3 Pippa wants to volunteer as a …   a nurse. ☐   b caregiver. ☐   c paramedic. ☐

4 For sports day, Marcus is going to compete in … a swimming. ☐   b tennis. ☐   c volleyball. ☐

5 Jessie's favorite subjects are …   a math. ☐   b science. ☐   c geography. ☐

3 Look at the lists of words (a–d). Which vocabulary group does each list belong to?

1 Where did Martin go on Saturday?

   a swimming pool   b park   c theater   d restaurant   _places in a town_

2 What did Monica's grandfather do when he was younger?

   a paramedic   b police officer   c vet   d firefighter   _____

3 What did Tim have after his accident?

   a bruises   b a cut head   c a broken leg   d a sprain   _____

4 How does Luke get to school?

   a bus   b on foot   c car   d bike   _____

5 What things does Mina have in her bedroom?

   a armchair   b closet   c desk   d wardrobe   _____

🎧 **4** Listen and choose the correct options in Exercise 3. You will hear all the options (a–d) mentioned,
E.03   but only two are correct.

GRAMMAR REFERENCE

Simple Present

Affirmative	Negative
I / You / We / They play the piano.	I / You / We / They do not (don't) play the piano.
He / She / It plays the piano.	He / She / It does not (doesn't) play the piano.

- We use the simple present to talk about facts, habits, and routines.
  I speak Italian.   He goes to college.
- The third person form (*he / she / it*) of the simple present ends in **-s**.
  eat – he eats   read – she reads
- With verbs ending in **consonant** + **-y**, we replace the **-y** with **-ies** for the *he / she / it* forms.
  study – she studies
- The *he / she / it* form of verbs ending in **-ss**, **-sh**, **-ch**, **-x**, and **-o** is **-es**.
  kisses finishes teaches relaxes goes
- Some verbs have an irregular spelling in the third person.
  have – she has   be – he is
- We form the negative of the simple present with the **subject** + **don't**/**doesn't** + **infinitive**.
  They don't speak Italian.
- We use **doesn't** in the third person (*he / she / it*).
  He doesn't play on the school team.

Questions	Short Answers
Do I / you / we / they like soccer?	Yes, I / you / we / they do. No, I / you / we / they don't.
Does he / she / it like soccer?	Yes, he / she / it does. No, he / she / it doesn't.

- We form simple present **Yes**/**No** questions with **do**/**does** + **subject** + **infinitive**.
  Do you read magazines?
- We use short answers with **do**/**does** to reply. We don't repeat the main verb.
  A: Do you write a blog? B: Yes, I do. (NOT *Yes, I write.*)

Adverbs of Frequency

never   sometimes   often   usually   always
0% ←——————————————————————→ 100%

- Adverbs of frequency say how often we do something. They go after the verb **to be** but before all other verbs.
  She's always late.   He sometimes chats online.
- In questions, adverbs of frequency always come after the subject.
  Do you always watch TV online?

Love, Like, Don't Mind, Hate + -ing

- We use the **-ing** form of the verb after **like**, **don't like**, **don't mind**, **love**, and **hate**.
  She loves making cakes. (NOT *She loves make cakes.*)
- We can also use nouns after these verbs.
  He doesn't mind basketball, but he loves tennis.

To Have

Affirmative	Negative
I / You / We / They have a phone.	I / You / We / They do not (don't) have a phone.
He / She / It has a phone.	He / She / It does not (doesn't) have a phone.

- We use **have** to talk about possession and relationships.
  I have five brothers.
- We usually use contractions in conversation.
  He doesn't have any cousins.
- We use the full form to be more formal.
  He does not have any cousins.
- To make the negative, we put **n't** (*not*) after **do** and before **have**.
  We don't have a portable charger.

Questions	Short Answers
Do I / you / we / they have a laptop?	Yes, I / you / we / they do. No, I / you / we / they don't.
Does he / she / it have a laptop?	Yes, he / she / it does. No, he / she / it doesn't.

- We use **do** + **subject** + **have** + **object** in questions.
  Do you have headphones?
- In spoken English, we reply to questions with short answers.
  A: Do you have a tablet?
  B: Yes, I do. (NOT *Yes, I do have.*) / *No, I don't.* (NOT *No, I don't have.*)

GRAMMAR PRACTICE

Simple Present

1 Complete the table with the verbs in the box in the third person.

> fly   get up   go   ~~play~~   try   watch

-s	-es	-ies
1 ____plays____	3 _____	5 _____
2 _____	4 _____	6 _____

2 Complete the sentences with the simple present form of the verbs in parentheses.

1 Marta and Matt ___like___ sports. (like)
2 I do my homework during the week, but my best friend _____ it on Sundays. (do)
3 They _____ hockey on Saturdays. (play)
4 My sister _____ English in college. (study)
5 My dad _____ the bus to work every day. (catch)

3 Write sentences with the simple present.

1 I / not like / swimming
   I don't like swimming.
2 Harry / read / the school magazine / every week
   _____
3 My sister / not hang out / with friends in the evening
   _____
4 My friends / love / my new blog
   _____
5 Laura and Luis / not play / hockey on Saturdays
   _____
6 We / do / homework / at the homework club
   _____

4 Write *Yes/No* questions and short answers.

1 Molly / get up / at 6 a.m. / every day / ? (✓)
   Does Molly get up at 6 a.m. every day?   *Yes, she does.*
2 Dan / read / your blog / ? (✗)
   _____   _____
3 you / play computer games / with your friends / ? (✓)
   _____   _____
4 your sister / write / good stories / ? (✗)
   _____   _____
5 Ruth and Ben / go to / the same school / ? (✓)
   _____   _____

Adverbs of Frequency

5 Circle the correct options.

1 Carlos *always does* / *does always* his homework in front of the TV.
2 They *often are* / *are often* at the park on the weekend.
3 Gina and Martin *usually go* / *go usually* to the movies on Saturdays.
4 I *sometimes get* / *get sometimes* DVDs from the library.
5 My sister *never is* / *is never* late for school.
6 Alex *usually listens* / *listens usually* to music in the evening.

Love, Like, Don't Mind, Hate + -ing

6 Write sentences with *love*, *like*, *don't mind*, *hate + -ing*.

1 I / love / watch / movies
   I love watching movies.
2 Molly / not mind / get up / early
   _____
3 We / like / go / to the gym
   _____
4 My dad / hate / listen / to the radio
   _____
5 Jen / not mind / do / homework
   _____

To Have

7 Complete the text with the correct form of *have*.

I ¹ ___have___ a new friend. Her name's Isabel. She ² _____ brown hair and blue eyes. She ³ _____ (not) any brothers, but she ⁴ _____ three sisters. Her mom and dad ⁵ _____ a house next to ours! I really like her because we ⁶ _____ the same hobbies, and we like the same things! What about you? ⁷ _____ you _____ a good friend in your class? ⁸ _____ your friend _____ the same hobbies as you?

GRAMMAR REFERENCE & PRACTICE 87

GRAMMAR REFERENCE

Present Continuous

Affirmative	Negative
I am ('m) watching TV.	I am ('m) not watching TV.
You / We / They are ('re) watching TV.	You / We / They are not (aren't) watching TV.
He / She / It is ('s) watching TV.	He / She / It is not (isn't) watching TV.

- We use the present continuous to talk about actions in progress at the time of speaking.
  You are learning about the present continuous.

- For the affirmative, we use **subject** + **be** + **infinitive** + **-ing**.
  Tom's watching a reality show. *We're reading a blog.*

- For the negative, we put **not** after **be**.
  She is not (isn't) downloading songs.

Questions	Short Answers
Am I watching TV?	Yes, I am. No, I'm not.
Are you / we / they watching TV?	Yes, you / we / they are. No, you / we / they aren't.
Is he / she / it watching TV?	Yes, he / she / it is. No, he / she / it isn't.

- To form questions, we use **be** + **subject** + **infinitive** + **-ing**.
  Are you watching cartoons?

- We don't use the **infinitive** + **-ing** in short answers.
  Yes, I am. (NOT *Yes, I am watching.*)

- We form information questions with a **Wh-** question word before *be*.
  Who are you reading about?
  What are you watching on TV?

- With most verbs, we add **-ing** to the **infinitive**.
  speak – speaking   read – reading   drink – drinking

- For verbs ending in **-e**, we remove the **-e** and add **-ing**.
  write – writing   have – having   give – giving

- For verbs ending in a vowel and a consonant, we double the final consonant and add **-ing**.
  stop – stopping   shop – shopping   plan – planning

Simple Present and Present Continuous

- We use the simple present to talk about facts, habits, and routines.
  Water freezes at 0 °C.
  I listen to music when I walk to school.
  She always goes shopping on Fridays.

- We use the present continuous to talk about actions in progress at the time of speaking.
  I watch a lot of TV. At the moment, I'm watching a great streaming series.
  He usually works in an office, but he's working at home today.

- Some verbs are not usually used in the continuous form: **know**, **understand**, **like**, **love**, **prefer**, **hate**, **need**, **remember**, **think**, **want**.
  I like this show. (NOT *I'm liking this show.*)

- We use expressions like **at the moment** and **right now** with the present continuous.
  He's doing his homework at the moment.

- We use adverbs of frequency with the simple present.
  He always does his homework after dinner.

Adverbs of Manner

- We use adverbs of manner to say how we do something.
  Carl can run very fast.

- Adverbs of manner come after the verb or the object if the sentence contains one.
  They don't speak clearly.
  Lia can draw animals well.

- To form regular adverbs, we add **-ly** to the adjective.
  nice – nicely   loud – loudly

- For adjectives ending in **-y**, we remove the **-y** and add **-ily**.
  happy – happily   noisy – noisily

- For adjectives ending in **-l**, we add **-ly**.
  careful – carefully   beautiful – beautifully

- Some adverbs of manner are irregular.
  good – well   hard – hard   late – late

GRAMMAR PRACTICE

Present Continuous

1 Complete the chart with the verbs in the *-ing* form.

~~do~~ run shop take walk write

Add *-ing*	Remove the -e and Add *-ing*	Double the Consonant and Add *-ing*
1 _doing_	3 _____	5 _____
2 _____	4 _____	6 _____

2 Complete the sentences with the present continuous form of the verbs in parentheses.

1 My best friends _are reading_ in the library. (read)

2 I _____ for a new camera. (look)

3 My mom _____ in the café. (sit)

4 She _____ coffee. (not drink)

5 My dad _____ a chocolate cake in the kitchen. (make)

6 Rosie and Dan _____ online. (not chat)

3 Write present continuous questions and short answers about the people in the chart.

	Watch a Movie	Study Grammar
Jack	(1) ✗	(4) ✓
Rory and Holly	(2) ✓	(5) ✗
Alicia	(3) ✗	(6) ✓

1 _Is Jack watching a movie?_
  No, he isn't.

2 _____

3 _____

4 _____

5 _____

6 _____

Simple Present and Present Continuous

4 Put the words in the correct order to make sentences in the simple present or present continuous.

1 isn't / She / documentary / watching / the
  She isn't watching the documentary.

2 makes / My mom / always / for the show / the costumes
  _____

3 English / We / studying / aren't / today
  _____

4 to / the / best friend / to go / doesn't / want / movies / My
  _____

5 weekend / I / with / friends / on / the / chat / my / online
  _____

6 moment / I'm / helping / my / mom / the / at
  _____

5 Complete the sentences with the simple present or present continuous form of the verbs in the box.

listen make not do not talk visit ~~watch~~

1 We _'re watching_ a comedy show right now.

2 I _____ my homework at the moment.

3 They often _____ their aunt on Saturdays.

4 My grandma usually _____ to the news on the radio in the morning.

5 My mom sometimes _____ the food we see on cooking shows.

6 Ryan _____ on his phone to his best friend at the moment.

Adverbs of Manner

6 Complete the text with the adverb form of the adjectives in parentheses.

My brother doesn't make friends [1] _easily_ (easy). He only has two really good friends. They usually play computer games at home. I don't play with them because they do everything really [2] _____ (quick), and I play [3] _____ (slow) and [4] _____ (bad)!
My brother loves drawing, and he can draw [5] _____ (good). Sometimes he teaches me how to draw. I think he's a good teacher because he explains everything [6] _____ (careful).

Simple Past

Affirmative	Negative
I / You / He / She / It / We / They went to a museum.	I / You / He / She / It / We / They did not (didn't) go to a museum.

To Be	
I / He / She / It was bored.	I / He / She / It was not (wasn't) bored.
You / We / They were bored.	You / We / They were not (weren't) bored.

- We use the simple past to talk about completed events and actions in the past.
  He watched a history documentary last night.
  We were tired after the trip.
- Most verbs in the simple past end in **-ed**.
  want – wanted   need – needed   show – showed
- For verbs ending in **-e**, add **-d**.
  live – lived   hate – hated   practice – practiced
- For verbs ending **consonant** + **-y**, we remove the **-y** and add **-ied**.
  study – studied   carry – carried   marry – married
- For verbs ending **consonant** + **vowel** + **consonant**, we double the final consonant and add **-ed**.
  shop – shopped   chat – chatted   stop – stopped
- Some simple past verbs are irregular.
  become – became   come – came   put – put
- See the irregular verbs list on page 111.

- To form the simple past negative, we use **subject** + **did not (didn't)** + **infinitive** without **to**.
  Mario didn't finish his homework last night.
- To form the past negative of **be**, add **not (n't)**.
  Mom wasn't very happy about my exam scores.

Questions	Short Answers
Did I / you / he / she / it / we / they go to a museum?	Yes, I / you / he / she / it / we / they did. No, I / you / he / she / it / we / they didn't.

To Be	
Was I / he / she / it bored?	Yes, I / he / she / it was. No, I / he / she / it wasn't.
Were you / we / they bored?	Yes, you / we / they were. No, you / we / they weren't.

- To form simple past questions, we use **Did** + **subject** + **infinitive** without **to**.
  Did Tom enjoy the concert yesterday?
- We put question words before **did**.
  What did you do last weekend?
- To form past questions with **be**, change the word order.
  Were you late to class this morning?

There Was/Were

	Affirmative	Negative
Singular	There was a bowl / some food.	There was not (wasn't) a bowl / any food.
Plural	There were some forks.	There were not (weren't) any forks.

- We use **there was** and **there were** to talk about what existed in the past.
- We use **there was** with singular countable and uncountable nouns.
  There was a book here.   There was milk in the cup.
- We use **there were** with plural countable nouns.
  There were a lot of tourists in our town last weekend.
- We use **some** after **there was**/**were** with uncountable and plural countable nouns.
  There was some water in the bottle.
  There were some houses here years ago.
- We use **any** after **there wasn't**/**weren't** with uncountable and plural countable nouns.
  There wasn't any money in the purse.
  There weren't any cups.

	Questions	Short Answers
Singular	Was there a bowl / any food?	Yes, there was. No, there wasn't.
Plural	Were there any forks?	Yes, there were. No, there weren't.

- In questions, we usually use **any** with uncountable and plural countable nouns.
  Was there any bread at home?
  Were there any interesting objects at the museum?
- We don't repeat **any** in short answers.
  A: *Was there any news about Laura?*
  B: *No, there wasn't.* (NOT ~~No, there wasn't any~~.)

GRAMMAR PRACTICE

Simple Past

1 Complete the chart with the simple past form of the verbs in the box.

> cry   like   plan   smile   stay   stop   study   ~~wait~~

Add -ed	Ending in -e, Add -d	Remove -y, Add -ied	Double Final Consonant, Add -ed
1 _waited_	3 _____	5 _____	7 _____
2 _____	4 _____	6 _____	8 _____

2 Write sentences with the simple past.

1 Tom / wait / three hours / for the train
   Tom waited three hours for the train.

2 Joanna / not go / to school / last week
   _____

3 Megan and Sarah / not feel / tired after the trip
   _____

4 The trip / take / ten hours!
   _____

5 I / buy / some / new shoes
   _____

3 Write simple past questions and short answers about the people in the chart.

	Beth	Maria and Sam	Ivan
go movies	(1) ✗	(3) ✓	(5) ✓
eat pizza	(2) ✓	(4) ✗	(6) ✗

1 Did Beth go to the movies?
   No, she didn't.

2 _____

3 _____

4 _____

5 _____

6 _____

4 Complete the question for each answer.

1 A: What _did you drink?_
   B: I drank some soda.

2 A: Where _____?
   B: He went to a concert.

3 A: When _____?
   B: They started school in January.

4 A: Who _____?
   B: She met her sister.

5 A: What _____?
   B: He ate a hotdog.

6 A: Why _____?
   B: They stayed at home because it was foggy.

There Was/Were

5 Complete the text with *there was(n't)/were(n't)*.

When I was in elementary school, [1] _there weren't_ a lot of exams and [2] _____ a lot of students in my class – I think [3] _____ only nine or ten of us. In my classroom, [4] _____ an internet connection or an electronic board, but my classroom was beautiful. [5] _____ pictures and stories on the walls, and [6] _____ a storytelling hour every day. [7] _____ any computers or laptops in our class in those days, but we loved writing on the board!

6 (Circle) the correct options.

1 Were there *a / some / (any)* posters on the walls?
2 There wasn't *an / some / any* exam every week.
3 There weren't *a / some / any* computers.
4 Was there *a / some / any* board in the classroom?
5 There wasn't *a / some / any* window in the classroom.
6 There were *an / some / any* interesting storybooks.

7 Complete the questions with *Was there* or *Were there*.

1 _Were there_ many people at the party?
2 _____ any good TV shows on last night?
3 _____ a party at your house last night?
4 _____ an exam at school last week?
5 _____ three or four students at the library?

Past Continuous: Affirmative and Negative

Affirmative	Negative
I / He / She / It was traveling.	I / He / She / It was not (wasn't) traveling.
You / We / They were traveling.	You / We / They were not (weren't) traveling.

- We use the past continuous to talk about actions in progress at a specific time in the past, or actions interrupted by another action.
  We were doing homework at 5 p.m. yesterday.
  Chloe was reading when James texted her.
- We form affirmative sentences with **subject** + **was**/**were** + **infinitive** + **-ing**.
  He was walking to school.
- To form the negative, we put **n't** (**not**) after **was**/**were** and before the **infinitive** + **-ing**. **Not** is usually contracted.
  They weren't listening to the teacher.

Past Continuous: Questions

Questions	Short Answers
Was I / he / she / it traveling?	Yes, I / he / she / it was. No, I / he / she / it wasn't.
Were you / we / they traveling?	Yes, you / we / they were. No, you / we / they weren't.

- We form questions with **Was**/**Were** + **subject** + **infinitive** + **-ing**.
  Were you reading in bed last night?
- We don't use **infinitive** + **-ing** in short answers.
  A: Was he chatting online?
  B: Yes, he was. (NOT Yes, he was chatting.)
- For information questions, we put the **Wh-** question word before **be**.
  What were you doing this morning?

Simple Past and Past Continuous

- We often use the simple past and past continuous together. We use the simple past for shorter actions that interrupt longer actions in the past continuous.

simple past

↓

———————————————————————————→

past continuous

I was cycling to school when I saw Lily.
He was walking through the park when he fell and hurt his knee.

- We often use **when**, **while**, and **as** with the past continuous.
  Their computer broke when they were studying.
  While she was having breakfast, she got a text from Madeline.
  As we were leaving the party, Lucas arrived.
- We use **when** with the simple past for shorter actions.
  When I saw Tom, he was arguing with Adele in the street. (NOT While I saw Tom …)

GRAMMAR PRACTICE

Past Continuous: Affirmative and Negative

1 Complete the sentences with the past continuous form of the verbs in the box.

> chat   get   hide   ~~play~~   take   watch

At 5 p.m. yesterday afternoon …

1 Peter ___was playing___ the piano.
2 Hugo _____ a shower.
3 Finn and Olivia _____ with friends.
4 We _____ a drama series on TV.
5 My sister _____ dressed.
6 The children _____ under the bed!

2 Complete the sentences with the negative past continuous form of the verbs in parentheses.

1 Aaron ___wasn't playing___ soccer. (play)
2 Diana _____ emails. (write)
3 Kate and Denise _____ in the backyard. (sit)
4 We _____ our bikes. (ride)
5 I _____ a sandwich. (eat)
6 The children _____ any noise. (make)

Past Continuous: Questions

3 Write questions with the past continuous.

1 What / you / do / yesterday / ?
  ___What were you doing yesterday?___
2 Where / they / go / last night / ?
  _____
3 Who / she / talk to / ?
  _____
4 Why / he / laugh / at me / ?
  _____
5 Where / you and your mom / stay / ?
  _____
6 What / your / friends / say / ?
  _____

4 (Circle) the correct options.

1 **A:** Was he reading the story?
  B: Yes, he (was) / were.
2 **A:** Were they playing soccer at 4 p.m.?
  B: No, they was / weren't.
3 **A:** Were you talking on the phone to your friend at 10 p.m. last night?
  B: No, I wasn't / weren't.
4 **A:** Was your mom making breakfast at 7 a.m.?
  B: Yes, she was / were.
5 **A:** Were you watching TV at 9 p.m. yesterday?
  B: Yes, we was / were.
6 **A:** Was Susan doing her homework at 6 p.m.?
  B: Yes, she was / were.

Simple Past and Past Continuous

5 Complete each sentence with the simple past or the past continuous form of the verbs in parentheses.

1 While we ___were walking___ (walk) home, we _____saw_____ (see) eight or nine cats crossing the street!
2 He _____ (go) to bed when the phone _____ (ring).
3 I _____ (fall) down while I _____ (walk) to school.
4 When I _____ (arrive) home, my dad _____ (dance) in the kitchen!
5 As the man _____ (take) the money, the police _____ (arrive).
6 While I _____ (chat) online, my mom _____ (come) into my room to turn the light off.

6 Complete the story with the simple past or the past continuous form of the verbs in parentheses.

I ¹ ___was getting___ (get) into bed last night when I
² _____ (see) a light in the backyard.
While I ³_____ (go) downstairs,
I ⁴_____ (hear) someone outside!
I ⁵_____ (try) to close the door when my
dad ⁶_____ (shout), "Let me in! It's me, your dad!"

Could

Affirmative	Negative
I / You / He / She / It / We / They could swim.	I / You / He / She / It / We / They could not (couldn't) swim.

- We use **could/couldn't** to talk about ability and possibility in the past and to make a polite request.
  When I was four I could swim ten meters.
  He couldn't call earlier because he was at work.
- **Could** is the same for all persons. The third person (*he / she / it*) form doesn't end in **-s**.
  She could sing "Happy Birthday" in three languages.
- To form the negative, we put **n't** (**not**) after **could**.
  He couldn't pay for his college books.

Questions	Short Answers
Could I / you / he / she / it / we / they swim?	Yes, I / you / he / she / it / we / they could. No, I / you / he / she / it / we / they couldn't.

- To form questions, we change the order of **could** and the subject.
  Could you speak English in elementary school?

Comparative and Superlative Adjectives

Comparatives	
Short adjectives: *smart*	add **-er**: *smarter*
Short adjectives ending in vowel + consonant: *big*	double the final consonant and add **-er**: *bigger*
Adjectives ending in **-e**: *safe*	add **-r**: *safer*
Adjectives ending in **-y**: *easy*	remove the **-y** and add **-ier**: *easier*
Long adjectives: *interesting*	put **more** before the adjective: *more interesting*
Irregular adjectives *good bad*	*better worse*

- We use comparative adjectives to compare one thing or person with another.
- We use the verb **be** + **comparative adjective** + **than**.
  Riley is taller than Amelia.

Superlatives	
Short adjectives: *smart*	add **-est**: *the smartest*
Short adjectives ending in vowel + consonant: *big*	double the final consonant and add **-est**: *the biggest*
Adjectives ending in **-e**: *safe*	add **-st**: *the safest*
Adjectives ending in **-y**: *easy*	remove the **-y** and add **-iest**: *the easiest*
Long adjectives: *interesting*	put **the most** before the adjective: *the most interesting*
Irregular adjectives *good bad*	*the best the worst*

- We use superlative adjectives to say a thing or person has the most of a particular quality.
- We use **the** with a **superlative adjective**.
  Riley is the tallest person in her family.

Too, Too Much, Too Many

- We use **too**, **too much**, and **too many** to say that there is an excess of something.
- We use **too** with **adjectives**.
  I'm too excited to sleep – it's my birthday tomorrow!
- We use **too much** with **uncountable nouns**.
  I have too much homework, so I can't go out tonight.
- We use **too many** with **plural countable nouns**.
  Daniel has too many plans for the weekend – he doesn't know which one to choose.

(Not) Enough + Noun

- We use **enough** when we have the right amount of something or something is sufficient.
  My brother has enough experience to work there.
- We use **not enough** when we need more of something or something is insufficient.
  I don't have enough time to do volunteer work on the weekend.

GRAMMAR PRACTICE

Could

1 Complete the sentences with *could* or *couldn't* and the verb in parentheses.

1 I ___could speak___ French when I was five. (speak)

2 She _____ a shower because there wasn't any water. (not take)

3 My grandparents _____ a house when they were young because they were poor. (not buy)

4 Tyler _____ all the questions on his English test because they were easy. (answer)

5 We _____ him because he spoke very quietly. (not hear)

6 Lynn _____ a bike when she was six, but I couldn't. (ride)

2 Put the words in the correct order to make questions with *could*.

1 five / read / Could / were / you / when / you / ?
Could you read when you were five?

2 his / brother / Could / Spanish / speak / ?
_____

3 his / understand / Amy and David / accent / Could / ?
_____

4 six / Jeff / skate / was / he / when / Could / ?
_____

5 yesterday / you / understand / Could / science / the / class / ?
_____

Comparative and Superlative Adjectives

3 Complete the sentences with the comparative form of the adjectives in parentheses.

1 Math is ___more boring___ (boring) than history.

2 Ava's homework is _____ (good) than Tim's homework.

3 Our new house is _____ (big) than the old one.

4 The weather in December is _____ (bad) than the weather in August.

5 I think my brother is _____ (intelligent) than me.

4 Circle the correct options.

1 A: I think being a firefighter is *more dangerous / the most dangerous* job in the world!

   B: I don't agree. I think a police officer's job is *more dangerous / the most dangerous* than a firefighter's job.

2 A: What is the *best / better* way to travel?

   B: People think it's traveling by plane, but I think going by train is *better / the best* than traveling by plane.

3 A: I think history is *easier / the easiest* subject.

   B: I don't agree. I think science is *easier / the easiest* than history.

Too, Too Much, Too Many; (Not) Enough + Noun

5 Put the words in the correct order to make sentences.

1 to / go / to / I'm / too / park / busy / the
I'm too busy to go to the park.

2 work / My / too / mom / has / much
_____

3 clothes / have / I / too / in / many / wardrobe / my
_____

4 enough / don't have / money / I / buy / to / a / new laptop
_____

5 doesn't have / enough / to / study / She / time
_____

6 Complete the text with the words in the box.

> enough   not enough   too (x2)
> too many   too much

I went to my first concert last week. I didn't like it. It was [1] ___too___ noisy, and there were [2] _____ people there. I wanted to have something to eat, but there was [3] _____ food for everybody. After two hours, I was [4] _____ hungry to stay and asked my mom to take me home. When we arrived home, Dad had [5] _____ work and didn't have [6] _____ time to cook dinner, so we had pizza and then I went to bed!

(Not) As … As

- We use (**not**) **as** … **as** to compare one thing or person with another.
  This tablet is as expensive as a laptop.
- We use **not as** + **adjective** + **as** to say that two things or people are not equal in some way.
  Being a nurse isn't as dangerous as being a firefighter.
  (= Being a firefighter is more dangerous than being a nurse.)
- We use **as** + **adjective** + **as** to say two things or people are the same.
  Being a nurse is as hard as being a doctor. (= Being a doctor is as hard as being a nurse.)

(Not) … Enough

- We use **not** + **adjective** + **enough** when we need more of something or something is insufficient.
  I'm not old enough to drive a car. I'm only 15.
- We use **adjective** + **enough** when we have the right amount of something or something is sufficient.
  This carpet is big enough to cover the floor.

Have To

Affirmative	Negative
I / You / We / They have to do the ironing.	I / You / We / They do not (don't) have to do the ironing.
He / She / It has to do the ironing.	He / She / It does not (doesn't) have to do the ironing.

- We use **have to** to say that something is necessary.
  My sister has to empty the dishwasher every day.
  You have to drive on the right side of the road in the U.S.A.
- We use **don't have to** to say that something isn't necessary.
  I don't have to help at home, but it makes my parents happy.
  They don't have to do after-school activities at their school.

Questions	Short Answers
Do I / you / we / they have to do the ironing?	Yes, I / you / we / they do. No, I / you / we / they don't.
Does he / she / it have to do the ironing?	Yes, he / she / it does. No, he / she / it doesn't.

- To form questions, we use **Do/Does** + **subject** + **have to** + **infinitive**.
  Does your mom have to work on the weekend?
- In short answers we repeat **do** or **does**, not **have to**.
  A: Do you have to go to bed early during the week?
  B: Yes, I do. (NOT ~~Yes, I have to.~~)

(Not) As … As

1 Complete the second sentence so it has the same meaning as the first sentence. Use (*not*) *as … as* and the adjectives in parentheses.

1 Her new computer is smaller than her old computer.

Her old computer ___isn't as small as___ her new computer. (small)

2 This red carpet is the same size as the blue one.

This red carpet _____ the blue one. (big)

3 This chest of drawers is prettier than my wardrobe.

My wardrobe _____ this chest of drawers. (beautiful)

4 These armchairs are the same price as the chairs.

The chairs _____ the armchairs. (expensive)

5 This camera is lighter than my smartphone.

My smartphone _____ this camera. (light)

6 The rooms in our apartment are wider than the rooms in your apartment.

The rooms in your apartment _____ the rooms in our apartment. (wide)

(Not) … + Enough

2 Match 1–5 with a–e.

1 My bedroom is too small. `d`
2 You're too young. ☐
3 My shoes are too dirty. ☐
4 This game is too easy. ☐
5 It's too cold to go swimming. ☐

a It isn't difficult enough.
b You aren't enough.
c The weather isn't hot enough.
d It isn't big enough.
e They aren't clean enough to wear to school!

3 Complete the text with the phrases in the box.

> as big as   as comfortable as   as small as
> ~~as wide as~~   big enough

I got a new bed last week because I wanted a big, comfortable bed that was [1] _as wide as_ my parents' bed. We bought one that was [2] _____ for five people to sleep in! My bedroom isn't [3] _____ my parents' room (theirs is huge), and it's also smaller than my brother's, so my new bed is too big for my room. I sleep well in the bed because it's [4] _____ my parents' bed, but I can't have any furniture in my room now! My brother wants the new bed because he says his room isn't [5] _____ mine, so there's more space! No way!

Have To

4 Complete the sentences with the correct form of *have to*.

1 My teacher ___has to___ correct a lot of homework. ✓
2 To send a text message, you _____ have a cell phone. ✓
3 My brother _____ go to school by bus because my dad takes him in the car. ✗
4 David and Maria _____ do a lot of homework on the weekend. ✗
5 They _____ wear uniforms at my sister's school. ✓
6 We _____ cook dinner on Mondays and Fridays because Dad does it then. ✗

5 ⟨Circle⟩ the correct options.

1 Jake *has to* / ⟨*doesn't have to*⟩ wash the dishes because there's a dishwasher.
2 *Do* / *Does* Cindy and Tim have to clean the bathroom?
3 Kim *has to* / *doesn't have to* do the shopping because her parents are too busy.
4 Olly *has to* / *doesn't have to* wash his clothes by hand because there is a washing machine.
5 Mom and Dad *don't have to* / *have to* mop the floor because we do it.
6 **A:** *Do* / *Does* Lauren have to do any chores at home?
   B: Yes, she *do* / *does*.

GRAMMAR REFERENCE

Should/Shouldn't

Should/Shouldn't	
Affirmative	**Negative**
I / You / He / She / It / We / They should be careful on the beach.	I / You / He / She / It / We / They should not (shouldn't) swim in cold water.

- We use **should** and **shouldn't** to give advice and say that we think something is a good or bad idea.
  You should put cold water on a burn.
- **Should** doesn't change in the different persons. We use an **infinitive without to** after **should**.
  He should help his parents with the housework.

Must/Mustn't

Must/Mustn't	
Affirmative	**Negative**
I / You / He / She / It / We / They must drive on the left in the UK.	I / You / He / She / It / We / They must not (must not) swim when there is a red flag.

- We use **must** and **must not** to give strong advice and talk about rules.
  You must watch this TV show; it's great.
  You must be 17 to drive a car.
- **Must not** means that something isn't allowed.
  You mustn't use your phone in the theater.
- **Must** doesn't change in the different persons. We use an **infinitive without to** after **must**.
  He must remember to take his medicine every day.

Zero Conditional

Action/Situation: simple present	Result: simple present
If a bee stings you,	it hurts.
Result: simple present	**Action/Situation:** simple present
It hurts	if a bee stings you.

- We use the zero conditional to talk about situations and their results that are always true.
  If you heat water to 100 °C, it boils.
  When you sprain your ankle, it usually bruises.
- We use a comma to separate the two clauses when the action/situation clause comes first.
  If you work hard, you get results.

First Conditional

Action/Situation: simple present	Result: *will* + infinitive
If we see a jaguar,	we 'll take a photo.
Result: *will* + infinitive	**Action/Situation:** simple present
We'll take a photo	if we see a jaguar.

- We use the first conditional to talk about possible situations in the future and their results.
  If we pass all our exams, we'll have a party.
  You'll get cavities if you eat too much sugar.
- We use a comma to separate the two clauses if the action/situation clause comes first.
  If the weather is nice tomorrow, we'll go to the park.

GRAMMAR PRACTICE

Should/Shouldn't and Must/Mustn't

1 Complete the sentences with *should* or *shouldn't* and the verbs in the box.

> go (x2)   open   stay   wear (x2)

1 It's cold today. You ___should wear___ a warm coat.
2 People say there are sharks in the ocean. You _____ swimming.
3 It's raining. You _____ your umbrella.
4 I have an exam tomorrow. I _____ up too late.
5 **A:** I have a toothache.
   B: You _____ to the dentist.
6 **A:** These new shoes are too small for me.
   B: You _____ them!

2 Complete the sentences with *must* or *must not* and the verb in parentheses.

1 You _must not laugh_ at other students in class. (laugh)
2 You _____ early to get to school on time. (get up)
3 You _____ sandwiches in the classroom. It isn't allowed. (eat)
4 You _____ loudly in the theater. (talk)
5 You _____ on the chairs. (stand)
6 You _____ your teeth every day. (brush)

3 Complete the text with *must* or *must not* and the verbs in the box.

> climb   look   ~~swim~~   take   walk   wear

My grandma always thinks of the bad things that can happen to me! When I go to the beach, she says I [1] _must not swim_ in the ocean because it's dirty, I [2] _____ sandals on the beach because there's a lot of broken glass, and I [3] _____ out for sharks in the water! When I go to the mountains, she says I [4] _____ near animals that bite or sting, I [5] _____ my phone with me so she can call me, and I [6] _____ any mountains in case I break my leg!

Zero Conditional

4 Match 1–6 with a–f.

1 If it rains,   [c]
2 When you read books,   [ ]
3 If my friend is feeling sad,   [ ]
4 When a snake bites you,   [ ]
5 You make the color green   [ ]
6 If I don't understand something in class, [ ]

a I try to make her laugh.
b if you mix yellow and blue.
c the grass gets wet.
d you learn things.
e I ask my teacher for help.
f you need to go to the hospital.

First Conditional

5 (Circle) the correct options.

1 If (you go) / you'll go online, I / (I'll) show you my new website.
2 *We / We'll* learn which plants are dangerous if *we go / we'll go* to the classes.
3 If *they swim / they'll swim* in the ocean at night, *they are / they'll be* in danger.
4 If you *don't come / won't come*, *I'm not / I won't be* your friend anymore!
5 If *he sees / he'll see* a tarantula, *he's / he'll be* frightened!

6 Complete the conditional sentences with the correct form of the verbs in the box.

> call   eat   not go   not have   ~~take~~

1 If the computer doesn't work, I'll take _____ it to the store.
2 Sally will play games online if she _____ any homework.
3 They _____ us if they are late.
4 If Harry doesn't get the job, he _____ on vacation.
5 If you _____ something, you'll feel better.

Present Perfect: Affirmative and Negative

Affirmative	Negative
I / You / We / They have ('ve) finished.	I / You / We / They have not (haven't) finished.
He / She / It has ('s) finished.	He / She / It has not (hasn't) finished.

- We use the present perfect to talk about actions with a present result and actions within an unfinished time period.
  I've found my favorite hat!
  Logan hasn't been to the dentist this year.
- To form affirmative sentences, use **subject** + **have/has** + **past participle**.
  I've burned my hand.
- To form negative sentences, we put **n't** (**not**) after **have/has** and before the past participle. **Not** is usually contracted.
  Smartphones haven't replaced human interaction completely.
- Most verbs in the past participle form end in **-ed**.
  want – wanted   need – needed   play – played
- For verbs ending in **-e**, add **-d**.
  love – loved   hope – hoped   live – lived
- For verbs ending in **consonant** + **-y**, remove the final **-y** and add **-ied**.
  study – studied   try – tried   copy – copied
- For verbs ending in **consonant** + **vowel** + **consonant**, double the final consonant and add **-ed**.
  slip – slipped   shop – shopped   drop – dropped
- Some past participles are irregular and don't follow any pattern.
  see – seen   find – found   put – put
- See the irregular verbs list on page 111.

Will/Won't, May, and Might

Will/Won't	
Affirmative	**Negative**
I / You / He / She / It / We / They will ('ll) survive.	I / You / He / She / It / We / They will not (won't) survive.

- We use **will** and **won't** to make certain predictions about the future.
  Computers will control our lives in the future.
  The laptop will help me with my homework.

Will/Won't	
Questions	**Short Answers**
Will I / you / he / she / it / we / they survive?	Yes, I / you / he / she / it / we / they will. No, I / you / he / she / it / we / they won't.

- To form questions, we change the order of **will** and the subject.
  Will we travel in cars in the future?

May and Might	
Affirmative	**Negative**
I / You / He / She / It / We / They may have a flying car.	I / You / He / She / It / We / They may not have a flying car.
I / You / He / She / It / We / They might have a flying car.	I / You / He / She / It / We / They might not have a flying car.

- We use **may** and **might** to make uncertain predictions about the future.
  Rhinos may become extinct in the future; no one knows for sure.
  I might go to Bridget's house this weekend; I don't know yet.

Infinitive of Purpose

- We use **to** + **infinitive** to express a purpose for doing something.
  I use a car to get to work.
  She bought a tablet to watch videos when she travels.
  They saved money to pay for the wedding.
  (NOT ~~They saved money for pay for the wedding.~~)

GRAMMAR PRACTICE

Present Perfect: Affirmative and Negative

1 Complete the chart with the past participle of the verbs in the box.

change	drop	plan	study	try	~~upload~~

Add -*d* or -*ed*	Remove -*y*, Add -*ied*	Double Final Consonant, Add -*ed*
1 _uploaded_	3 _____	5 _____
2 _____	4 _____	6 _____

2 Write the past participle of the verbs.

1 have ___had___   4 write _____
2 do _____   5 forget _____
3 ride _____   6 see _____

3 Complete the sentences with the correct form of *have*.

1 I _'ve___ joined an online club at school.
2 Ava _____ fallen off her bike.
3 Luke _____ broken his wrist.
4 We _____ sent them a message.
5 My brother _____ won an internet competition.
6 Laptops _____ made homework easier!

4 Complete the sentences with the present perfect form of the verbs in parentheses.

1 I think I_'ve lost___ my new phone. (lose)
2 I can't use my laptop because I _____ my password! (forget)
3 My brother _____ his bed this morning. (not make)
4 Ruth _____ her ankle! (break)
5 My grandpa _____ a new computer! (buy)
6 My teacher says smartphones _____ how we speak to each other. (change)

Will/Won't, May, and Might

5 Complete the text with *will* and the verbs in the box.

be (x2)	do	~~go~~	study	work

In the future, I think I [1]_'ll go___ to college, and I [2]_____ computer technology. I think that computer technology [3]_____ very important in the future because there [4]_____ a lot of new developments in science and technology. Then I think I [5]_____ research at a university in the U.S.A. or Australia. After that, I think I [6]_____ at a company which invents new technology.

6 (Circle) the correct options.

1 In the future, children *will* / (*won't*) go to school because they'll study at home.
2 Quinn *might* / *will* be in his bedroom, but I don't know. Go and look.
3 We *will* / *won't* all have electric cars in 100 years because there won't be any gasoline.
4 I *will* / *may* meet Tom tonight, but I haven't decided yet.
5 The library *won't* / *may not* let you borrow more than four books – I'm not sure. Let's ask.
6 People won't work in factories in the future because robots *will* / *won't* do all of the work.

Infinitive of Purpose

7 Complete the text with the infinitive of purpose. Use the verbs in the box.

~~buy~~	change	have	show	speak	take

Yesterday, my mom went shopping [1]_to buy___ a new smartphone. I went with her [2]_____ my new tablet for a different one because it was broken. When we were going home, we stopped at a café [3]_____ some coffee and then we stopped again [4]_____ to some neighbors we saw at the park. Mom used her new phone [5]_____ some photos of us [6]_____ my dad at home. It was really late when we got home, but my dad loved the photos!

Present Perfect for Experience

Affirmative	Negative
I / You / We / They have ('ve) seen this movie.	I / You / We / They have not (haven't) seen this movie.
He / She / It has ('s) seen this movie.	He / She / It has not (hasn't) seen this movie.

- We use the present perfect to talk about experiences.
  He's visited every country in Europe.
  Jayden and Layla haven't met Mia.

Questions	Short Answers
Have I / you / we / they seen this movie?	Yes, I / you / we / they have. No, I / you / we / they haven't.
Has he / she / it seen this movie?	Yes, he / she / it has. No, he / she / it hasn't.

- We form **Yes/No** questions with **have/has** + **subject** + **past participle**.
  Has your mom been to Spain?
- We repeat **have/has** in short answers.
  A: *Have you tried Portuguese food?*
  B: *Yes, I have.*

- When we talk about experience, we can use **ever** in questions to mean "at any time," and **never** in affirmative sentences to mean "at no time."
  Have you ever seen a crocodile in real life?
  I've never traveled outside of my country.

Reflexive Pronouns

I – myself	I saw **myself** on TV.
you – yourself	You saw **yourself** on TV.
he – himself	He saw **himself** on TV.
she – herself	She saw **herself** on TV.
it – itself	It saw **itself** on TV.
we – ourselves	We saw **ourselves** on TV.
you (plural) – yourselves	You saw **yourselves** on TV.
they – themselves	They saw **themselves** on TV.

- We use reflexive pronouns when the subject and the object of a sentence are the same, or to emphasize the subject of an action.
  My dad talks to himself when he's nervous.
  I made dinner myself because Dad was late.
- The pronoun usually goes directly after the verb.
  We enjoyed ourselves at Liam's birthday party.
  (NOT ~~We enjoyed at Liam's birthday party ourselves.~~)

Indefinite Pronouns

	People	Things	Places
Some…: to talk about one person / thing / place in a positive sentence	**Someone / Somebody** called me earlier.	I want **something** to eat.	I want to go **somewhere** hot on vacation.
Every…: to talk about all people, things, or places	**Everyone / Everybody** likes chocolate.	**Everything** in your flat is beautiful.	I've been **everywhere** in Chicago.
Any…: to talk about one person, thing, or place in a negative sentence or question	I don't know **anyone / anybody** at this party.	I don't have **anything** to wear to the party.	I don't want to go **anywhere** tonight.
No…: to indicate no people, things, or places	**No one / Nobody** called me yesterday.	**Nothing** happened last night.	**Nowhere** is open for dinner tonight.

- We use indefinite pronouns to talk about people, things, and places without specifying those people, things, and places.
- Indefinite pronouns take a singular verb.
  Everyone is excited about the wedding. (NOT ~~Everyone are excited about the wedding.~~)
- We usually use an affirmative verb with **no one**, **nothing**, and **nowhere**.
  There's nothing to do here! (NOT ~~There isn't nothing to do here!~~)
- We usually use a negative verb with **anyone**, **anything**, and **anywhere**.
  I don't have anything to do today. (NOT ~~I've got anything to do today.~~)

GRAMMAR PRACTICE

Present Perfect for Experience

1 Complete the sentences with the correct words.

> 've   ever   has   have   haven't   never

1 I've_____ flown on a plane.

2 He's _____ been to Iceland, but he wants to go in the future.

3 A: _____ you ever ridden a camel?

  B: No, I _____ .

4 A: Has your grandpa _____ used a laptop?

  B: Yes, he _____ !

2 Write questions and short answers with the present perfect and *ever*.

1 you / climb / a mountain / ?

  Have you ever climbed a mountain?

  No, I _haven't_ .

2 Christina / sprain / her ankle / ?

  _____

  Yes, she _____ .

3 Tony / eat / Japanese food / ?

  _____

  No, he _____ .

4 your parents / travel / to a different country / ?

  _____

  No, they _____ .

5 your sister / learn / a new language / ?

  _____

  Yes, she _____ .

6 you / spend / too much money / ?

  _____

  Yes, I _____ .

3 Underline and correct one mistake in each sentence.

1 Have <u>ever you</u> driven a car? _you ever_

2 I've never invent anything! _____

3 Has your brother ever win a prize? _____

4 She haven't been to a different country. _____

5 I haven't never seen a waterfall. _____

Reflexive Pronouns

4 (Circle) the correct options.

1 She wrote the song (herself) / himself.

2 He only thinks about *herself* / *himself*.

3 People with talent usually believe in *yourself* / *themselves*.

4 My dad says we should always defend *ourselves* / *themselves*.

5 I taught *myself* / *himself* how to play chess.

6 The laptop switches *itself* / *himself* off when you stop using it.

5 Complete the sentences with the correct reflexive pronouns.

1 Do you like looking at ___yourself___ in the mirror?

2 Monica taught _____ to play the guitar.

3 I don't like taking photos of _____ because I look terrible in them!

4 These lights turn _____ on when it's dark.

5 Jack hurt _____ when he was climbing.

6 We enjoyed _____ at the concert.

Indefinite Pronouns

6 (Circle) the correct options.

1 *Someone* / (*No one*) lives in that house – the last family moved out two weeks ago.

2 There's *something* / *nothing* better than helping other people.

3 My uncle loves traveling. He's been *everywhere* / *nowhere* except Australia and New Zealand!

4 *Somewhere* / *Someone* told me it's better to dress well if you want to make a good impression.

5 I have *nothing* / *no one* to tell you.

6 She doesn't have *anywhere* / *nowhere* to stay when she begins her new job in Miami.

Going To

Affirmative	Negative
I am ('m) going to dance.	I am ('m) not going to dance.
You / We / They are ('re) going to dance.	You / We / They are not (aren't) going to dance.
He / She / It is ('s) going to dance.	He / She / It is not (isn't) going to dance.

- We use **going to** to talk about future plans and intentions.
  I'm going to work in another country in the future.
- To form the affirmative, we use **be** + **going to** + **infinitive**.
  We're going to travel around Europe before college.
- To form the negative, we use **be** + **not** + **going to** + **infinitive**.
  Ryan isn't going to study French in France.

Questions	Short Answers
Am I going to dance?	Yes, I am. No, I'm not.
Are you / we / they going to dance?	Yes, you / we / they are. No, you / we / they aren't.
Is he / she / it going to dance?	Yes, he / she / it is. No, he / she / it isn't.

- We form questions with **be** before the subject.
  Are they going to get married this year?
- We repeat **be** in short answers.
  A: Are you going to learn the keyboard?
  B: Yes, I am.

Will and Going To

- We use **will** for predictions and **going to** for future plans and intentions.
  Lidia will be the best singer in the school show.
  We're going to write the school play next year.

Present Continuous for Future

- We use the present continuous to talk about fixed arrangements in the future, especially plans we've agreed with other people.
  I'm meeting my friends at 8 p.m. tomorrow. We're seeing a concert.
  We're having lunch with my aunt next Saturday.
- We often use future time expressions such as **tonight**, **tomorrow**, **this weekend**, **this summer**, **next week**, **next month,** and **after class**/**school** with the present continuous for future.
  Aria and I are practicing for the school talent show this weekend.

Simple Present for Future

- We use the simple present to talk about scheduled events in the future.
  The concert starts at 10 p.m. tomorrow. It ends at midnight.
  My plane leaves tomorrow morning at nine.
  Their train arrives at 8:45 in the morning.
  Our summer vacation starts on June 24.

GRAMMAR PRACTICE

Going To

1 Complete the sentences with the correct form of *going to* and the verbs in the box.

> buy   not go   not work   perform   ~~study~~

1 I *'m going to study* music and dance in college.
2 Anne _____ in her dad's store this summer.
3 My brother _____ in a musical next week.
4 My parents _____ a new house next year.
5 We _____ to summer camp this year.

2 Write questions with *going to*. Use the words in parentheses.

1 What *are you going to do* (you / do) this summer?
2 Where _____ (Tina / work) next year?
3 When _____ (your parents / start) salsa classes?
4 What _____ (brother / do) on the weekend?
5 _____ (you / learn) the guitar next year?
6 _____ (your sister / buy) tickets for the pop concert tomorrow?

Will and Going To

3 Decide if the sentences are predictions or intentions. Then (circle) the best options.

1 I think you (will) / *are going to* need an umbrella today because it might rain.
2 We *will* / *are going to* buy the tickets tomorrow for the show.
3 They *will* / *are going to* watch ballroom dancing tomorrow night.
4 I think it *will* / *is going to* be difficult to find a good job in the future.
5 I'm sure you *will* / *are going to* pass the exam – with a bit of luck.

Present Continuous for Future

4 Write present continuous sentences about the people in the chart.

	Jess	**Marta and Adam**
tonight	(1) study for a test	(3) go out for pizza with their friends
this weekend	(2) watch ballet	(4) go to a concert

1 *Jess is studying for a test tonight.*
2 _____
3 _____
4 _____

5 Complete the conversation with the present continuous form of the verbs in the box.

> ~~do~~   go (x2)   have   make   meet

MIA   What ¹ *are you doing* tonight?
MASON   I ² _____ dinner at Josh's house at about six, but nothing after that. Why?
MIA   Anna and I ³ _____ skating at the park.
MASON   Sounds interesting. What time ⁴ _____ you _____ to the park?
MIA   Well, the first dancers are always there at eight, but I ⁵ _____ Anna at 7:30 in the café in front of the park first. Why don't you ask Josh to come, too?
MASON   He can't. He ⁶ _____ a video with his classmates for a school project.

Simple Present for Future

6 Complete the sentences with the simple present form of the verbs in parentheses.

1 The bus *leaves* at 3 p.m. this afternoon. (leave)
2 When _____ this year's opera season _____? (begin)
3 The tap dancing class tomorrow _____ for more than three hours! (last)
4 My brother _____ his first concert next week! (have)
5 The show _____ at about 10 p.m. (end)
6 When _____ the new theater _____? (open)

LANGUAGE BANK

STARTER

Vocabulary
Free Time and Hobbies

> a bike ride   a blog   books/magazines
> cookies/videos   friends   an instrument
> music   online   photos   shopping   songs

Sports

> basketball   gymnastics   hockey
> rugby   sailing   swimming   table tennis
> track and field   volleyball   windsurfing

Personal Possessions

> bus pass   camera   headphones   keys
> laptop   money   passport   phone
> portable charger   tablet

Grammar in Action
Simple Present
Adverbs of Frequency
Love, Like, Don't Mind, Hate + -ing
To Have

Writing
Useful Language
Using Commas and Apostrophes
We use apostrophes:
- for contractions / short forms: *name's*
- to show possession: *My cat's name is Tiger.*
We use commas to indicate a pause: *I live with my mom and dad, my grandma, and my cat.*

UNIT 1

Vocabulary
TV Shows

> cartoon   comedy   cooking show
> documentary   drama   game show
> reality show   soap opera   sports show
> streaming series   talk show   the news

Making Movies

> actor   camera operator   costume
> (digital) camera   director   lights
> makeup artist   script   set   sound engineer

Grammar in Action
Present Continuous
Simple Present and Present Continuous
Adverbs of Manner

Speaking
Everyday English
Actually …
It's really cool!
Let's see.
Well?

Useful Language
I prefer watching …
I'm not really into it/them.
It's great/good/not bad/awful.
What do you think of …?

Writing
Useful Language
Giving Similar or Contrasting Information
and to add similar information
but to show different information
or when there is a choice of two or more things

LANGUAGE BANK

UNIT 2

Vocabulary

The Weather

> cloudy   cold   dry   foggy   hot
> icy   rainy   snowy   stormy   sunny   warm
> wet   windy

Useful Objects

> blanket   bowl   comb   cup   fork
> hairbrush   knife   lamp   mirror   pillow
> plate   scissors   spoon   toothbrush

Grammar in Action

Simple Past
There Was/Were

Speaking

Everyday English

Nothing much.
Sounds good!
That's a shame.
You learn something new every day!

Useful Language

How was your weekend?
It was (OK/good/great/amazing/awful), thanks.
What about you?
What did you do?
What was the weather like?
Where did you stay?

Writing

Useful Language
Writing an Account of a Journey
At first, …
Finally, …
(He) set off on …
There were a lot of problems.

UNIT 3

Vocabulary

Adjectives of Feeling

> afraid   angry   bored   embarrassed
> excited   lonely   nervous   surprised   tired
> worried   upset

Prepositions of Movement

> across   along   between   down
> into   off   out of   over   past   through
> under   up

Grammar in Action

Past Continuous: Affirmative and Negative
Past Continuous: Questions
Simple Past and Past Continuous

Speaking

Everyday English

Go on.
No idea.
What a great story!
You're kidding!

Useful Language

Guess what happened (yesterday)?
It happened to …
Really?
That's amazing/incredible!
What was (he) doing (at) …?

Writing

Useful Language
Sequencing Words and Phrases
At first, …
In the afternoon, …
Suddenly, …
The next day, …
The next morning, …
The other day, …

LANGUAGE BANK

UNIT 4

Vocabulary
Money Verbs

> borrow   change   cost   earn
> lend   owe   pay   save   sell   spend

Caring Jobs

> caregiver   firefighter   garbage collector   lawyer
> lifeguard   nurse   paramedic   police officer
> preschool teacher   surgeon   vet   volunteer

Grammar in Action
Could
Comparative and superlative Adjectives
Too, Too Much, Too Many
(*Not*) *Enough* + Noun

Speaking
Everyday English
cute
I owe you one.
There you go.
What's up?

Useful Language
Could you do me a favor?
I'm sorry, I can't.
It depends.
Sure.
Would you mind … + -*ing* … ?

Writing
Useful Language
Giving Your Opinion
First of all, …
I believe that …
In my opinion, …
Personally, I think that …
In conclusion, …

UNIT 5

Vocabulary
Furniture

> armchair   bookcase   carpet   ceiling
> chest of drawers   cupboard   desk   floor
> fridge   picture   shelves   sink   wardrobe

Household Chores

> do the dishes   do the ironing   do the laundry
> dust (the furniture)   load/empty the dishwasher
> make the bed   mop the floor
> sweep the floor   vacuum (the carpet)

Grammar in Action
(*Not*) *As … As*
(*Not*) … *Enough*
Have To

Speaking
Everyday English
I'm not convinced.
It looks awesome!
Me neither.
Me too.

Useful Language
at the bottom/top
in the background
on the left/right
What's that … ?

Writing
Useful Language
Adding Information
also
as well
as well as
too

LANGUAGE BANK

UNIT 6

Vocabulary
Accidents and Injuries

> break bruise burn cut fall off
> get bitten get stung hit scratch
> slip sprain trip over

Parts of the Body

> cheek chest chin elbow
> forehead heel knee neck
> shoulder teeth toe wrist

Grammar in Action
Should/Shouldn't and *Must/Must not*
Zero Conditional and First Conditional

Speaking
Everyday English
Awesome
Buddies
I'll have a go at it.
Good job

Useful Language
How about … + *-ing* … ?
Make sure you don't …
Why don't you … ?
You should definitely …

Writing
Useful Language
Giving Advice
I'd say …
If you ask me, …
Make sure …
That's why …

UNIT 7

Vocabulary
Communication and Technology

> app chip device download emoji
> message screen social media
> software upload video chat

Getting Around

> catch/take get into get off
> get on get out of go by go on

Grammar in Action
Present Perfect: Affirmative and Negative
Will/Won't, *May*, and *Might*
Infinitive of Purpose

Speaking
Everyday English
Got it?
Like this?
Not quite.
That's it.

Useful Language
Before you start, …
It's really important that …
Make sure that …
Remember (not) to …

Writing
Useful Language
Giving Examples
For example,
For instance,
such as
Adding More Information
In addition, …
What's more, …

LANGUAGE BANK

UNIT 8

Vocabulary
Exceptional Jobs and Qualities

> athlete   businessman/businesswoman
> composer   engineer   inventor
> mathematician   scientist   writer

> creativity   determination   intelligence
> skill   strength   talent

Phrasal Verbs: Achievement

> come up with   give up
> keep up with   look up to   set up
> show off   take part in   work out

Grammar in Action
Present Perfect for Experience
Reflexive Pronouns
Indefinite Pronouns

Speaking
Everyday English
Tell me more.
that kind of thing
the main thing is
you know

Useful Language
I've learned the basics of …
I'm passionate about …
I've had plenty of experience of …
I've learned how to …

Writing
Useful Language
Talking about Achievements
after a lot of effort
How did I do it?
My advice to you is …
My greatest achievement is …

UNIT 9

Vocabulary
Musical Instruments and Genres

> bass   drums   guitar   keyboard
> microphone   saxophone   trumpet   violin

> classical   folk   hip-hop   jazz   reggae   rock

Dance Styles

> ballet dancing   ballroom dancing   breakdancing
> disco dancing   folk dance   modern dance
> salsa dancing   swing   tap dancing   Zumba

Grammar in Action
Going To
Will and *Going To*
Present Continuous for Future
Simple Present for Future

Speaking
Everyday English
all day long
Never mind.
That's no good.
That's too bad.
What are you up to?

Useful Language
Do you feel like …?
I'd love to, but …
(She's) welcome to …
Thanks for asking, though.
Would you like to …?

Writing
Useful Language
Writing a Review
All in all, …
If you love (dance), this (show) is a must-see.
I was impressed by …
On the downside, …
The highlight of the show is …

IRREGULAR VERBS

Infinitive	Simple Past	Past Participle
be	was / were	been
beat	beat	beaten
become	became	become
begin	began	begun
break	broke	broken
bring	brought	brought
build	built	built
burn	burned	burned
buy	bought	bought
catch	caught	caught
choose	chose	chosen
come	came	come
cost	cost	cost
cut	cut	cut
do	did	done
draw	drew	drawn
drink	drank	drunk
drive	drove	driven
eat	ate	eaten
fall	fell	fallen
feed	fed	fed
feel	felt	felt
fight	fought	fought
find	found	found
fly	flew	flown
forget	forgot	forgotten
get	got	gotten
give	gave	given
go	went	gone
grow	grew	grown
hang	hung	hung
have	had	had
hear	heard	heard
hide	hid	hidden
hit	hit	hit
hold	held	held
keep	kept	kept

Infinitive	Simple Past	Past Participle
know	knew	known
leave	left	left
lend	lent	lent
lose	lost	lost
make	made	made
meet	met	met
pay	paid	paid
put	put	put
read	read	read
ride	rode	ridden
ring	rang	rung
run	ran	run
say	said	said
see	saw	seen
sell	sold	sold
send	sent	sent
set	set	set
show	showed	shown
shut	shut	shut
sing	sang	sung
sit	sat	sat
sleep	slept	slept
speak	spoke	spoken
spend	spent	spent
stand	stood	stood
swim	swam	swum
take	took	taken
teach	taught	taught
tell	told	told
think	thought	thought
throw	threw	thrown
understand	understood	understood
wake	woke	woken
wear	wore	worn
win	won	won
write	wrote	written

ACKNOWLEDGEMENTS

The authors and publishers acknowledge the following sources of copyright material and are grateful for the permissions granted. While every effort has been made, it has not always been possible to identify the sources of all the material used, or to trace all copyright holders. If any omissions are brought to our notice, we will be happy to include the appropriate acknowledgements on reprinting and in the next update to the digital edition, as applicable.

Key: **SU** = Starter Unit, **U** = Unit.

Text

U2: Text about Dervla Murphy. Copyright © Eland Publishing Ltd. Reproduced with permission; **U8:** Text about Jacob Barnett. Copyright © Kristine Barnett. Reproduced with kind permission of Kristine Barnett; Text about Aaron Fotheringham. Copyright © WCMX International, LLC. Reproduced with permission; Text about Bethany Hamilton. Copyright © Bethany Hamilton. Reproduced with permission.

Photography

The following photographs are sourced from Getty Images.

SU: Westend61; Sharlotta/iStock/Getty Images Plus; Imgorthand/E+; Tetra Images; Denise Crew; gbh007/iStock/Getty Images Plus; **U1:** Compassionate Eye Foundation/DigitalVision; aluxum/E+; FatCamera/E+; Creative Crop/Photodisc; pagadesign/E+; Maurizio Cigognetti/Photographer's Choice; Pakorn Polachai/EyeEm; Alexandr Dubovitskiy/iStock/Getty Images Plus; tovovan/iStock/Getty Images Plus; kotomiti/iStock/Getty Images Plus; nidwlw/iStock/Getty Images Plus; Jeffrey Coolidge/DigitalVision; D'Franc Photography/Moment Open; Ariel Skelley/DigitalVision; Kevin Dodge/The Image Bank; Feverpitched/iStock/Getty Images Plus; Tetra Images; Gusztav Gallo/EyeEm; PeopleImages/iStock/Getty Images Plus; Science Photo Library; 36clicks/iStock/Getty Images Plus; LueratSatichob/DigitalVision Vectors; Elva Etienne/Moment; ollo/iStock Unreleased; JGI/Jamie Grill; drbimages/E+; Westend61; PhotoAlto/Odilon Dimier/PhotoAlto Agency RF Collections; **U2:** alubalish/iStock/Getty Images Plus; Imgorthand/E+; Tim Graham/The Image Bank; stephen johnson/iStock/Getty Images Plus; Rolf Bruderer; Daniel Friend/iStock/Getty Images Plus; Lars Thulin, Johner; Tetra Images; Layland Masuda/Moment Open; Rob Lewine; NUTAN/Gamma-Rapho; Tuomas Lehtinen/Moment Open; coco lang; jordieasy/iStock/Getty Images Plus; Lovely Edeza/EyeEm; RinoCdZ/E+; xenicx/iStock/Getty Images Plus; Caiaimage/Paul Bradbury; Leemage/Universal Images Group; Stígur Már Karlsson/Heimsmyndir/E+; **U3:** Betsie Van Der Meer/DigitalVision; Michael Echteld/Moment; @ Didier Marti/Moment; Table Mesa Prod./Photolibrary; Norbert Schaefer/Corbis; Maskot; Getty Images/Hero Images; Comstock/Stockbyte; Erik Von Weber/The Image Bank; Patrick Schwalb/Picture Press; yaoinlove/iStock/Getty Images Plus; Adriana Varela Photography/Moment; AJ_Watt/E+; Nico De Pasquale Photography/Moment; perets/iStock/Getty Images Plus; whitemay/iStock/Getty Images Plus; Pete Saloutos/Image Source; Cultura RM Exclusive/Alan Graf/Cultura Exclusive; krblokhin/iStock/Getty Images Plus; Jupiterimages/Goodshoot; mtreasure/iStock/Getty Images Plus; LeventKonuk/iStock/Getty Images Plus; **U4:** bluecinema/iStock/Getty Images Plus; Tanya St/iStock/Getty Images Plus; Lokibaho/iStock Unreleased; kali9/iStock/Getty Images Plus; Yellow Dog Productions/The Image Bank; Ljupco/iStock/Getty Images Plus; drbimages/E+; Photo_Concepts/Cultura; Juanmonino/iStock/Getty Images Plus; Comstock Images/Stockbyte; moodboard/Cultura; Jamie Kingham/Image Source; FangXiaNuo/E+; SDI Productions/E+; DGLimages/iStock/Getty Images Plus; rubberball; jabejon/iStock/Getty Images Plus; Terry Vine/DigitalVision; Marc Romanelli; **U5:** Dorling Kindersley; YangYin/E+; Jena Ardell/Moment; Julija Svetlova/EyeEm; Grant Faint/The Image Bank; clu/iStock/Getty Images Plus; De Agostini/Al Pagani/De Agostini Picture Library; Nongnuch Leelaphasuk/EyeEm; Sergey05/iStock/Getty Images Plus; Kate Davis/Dorling Kindersley; Bryngelzon/E+; JazzIRT/E+; Mark Griffin/EyeEm; Skadr/iStock/Getty Images Plus; acilo/iStock/Getty Images Plus; Elisa Bonomini/EyeEm; bluestocking/iStock/Getty Images Plus; Carol Yepes/Moment; Ridofranz/iStock/Getty Images Plus; Hero Images; TanyaLovus/iStock/Getty Images Plus; penkanya/iStock/Getty Images Plus; Simon Watson/The Image Bank; Juanmonino/E+; Mehmet Hilmi Barcin/iStock/Getty Images Plus; CiydemImages/iStock/Getty Images Plus; SolStock/E+; Hoxton/Martin Barraud; Westend61; PaulVinten/iStock/Getty Images Plus; **U6:** Pixel_Pig/E+; yuoak/DigitalVision Vectors; Roger Eritja/Oxford Scientific; Will & Deni McIntyre/The Image Bank Unreleased; D. Sharon Pruitt Pink Sherbet Photography/Moment; Siberian Photographer/iStock/Getty Images Plus; Janista/iStock/Getty Images Plus; Ecelop/iStock/Getty Images Plus; designalldone/DigitalVision Vectors; Evgenii_Bobrov/iStock/Getty Images Plus; Creative Crop/Photodisc; JackF/iStock/Getty Images Plus; AH86/iStock/Getty Images Plus; Hero Images; Andreas Strauss/LOOK-foto; Westend61; **U7:** aphichart/iStock/Getty Images Plus; Colin Hawkins/Stone; Westend61; Monkey Business Images; Andrew Bret Wallis/DigitalVision; yuoak/DigitalVision Vectors; beyhanyazar/iStock/Getty Images Plus; Ronnie Kaufman/DigitalVision; Bojan89/iStock/Getty Images Plus; Valeriy_G/iStock/Getty Images Plus; Eugenio Marongiu/Cultura; izusek/E+; BJI/Lane Oatey; Mlenny/E+; Francis Dean/Corbis News; kate_sept2004/E+; **U8:** D Dipasupil/WireImage; James Devaney/Getty Images Entertainment; Icon Sport; jabejon/iStock/Getty Images Plus; SDI Productions/E+; MikeCherim/iStock/Getty Images Plus; Vladimir Godnik; Image Source/DigitalVision; Getty Images/Caiaimage; Morsa Images/DigitalVision; piamphoto/iStock/Getty Images Plus; GUSTOIMAGES/Science Photo Library/Getty Images Plus; Sion Touhig/Getty Images News; Hill Street Studios/DigitalVision; Tatiana Mezhenina/iStock/Getty Images Plus; CHUYN/DigitalVision Vectors; Tyler D. Rickenbach/Aurora Photos; **U9:** Arthur Baensch/Corbis; Jon Feingersh Photography Inc/DigitalVision; urbancow/iStock/Getty Images Plus; Hill Street Studios/DigitalVision; kali9/E+; Education Images/Universal Images Group; Laures/iStock/Getty Images Plus; Cimmerian/E+; JackF/iStock/Getty Images Plus; Dorling Kindersley; Hemera Technologies/PhotoObjects.net; lcodacci/E+; Seamind Panadda/EyeEm; Gannet77/E+; SDI Productions/E+; Monkey Business Images; Inti St Clair; eclipse_images/E+; Rubberball/Nicole Hill; Erik Isakson; Ryan Smith/Corbis; Paul Bradbury/OJO Images; recep-bg/E+; Jena Ardell/Moment; PeopleImages/E+.

The following photographs are sourced from other libraries/sources.

U1: Currency Images are courtesy of the Bureau of Engraving and Printing; **U2:** Copyright © Eland Publishing Ltd.; **U8:** Copyright © Kristine Barnett; Copyright © Bethany Hamilton; Copyright © WCMX International, LLC.

Illustration

U2, U3: Oliver Flores; **U3, U5, U6:** Alex Herrerias; **U3, U8, U9:** Jose Rubio; **U4, U7, U8, VE5:** Antonio Cuesta.

Typesetting: Aphik, S.A. de C.V.

Cover design and illustrations: Collaborate Agency

Audio Recordings: Eastern Sky Studios

American English Consultant: Anna Norris

Freelance Editors: Sue Costello, Jacqueline French, Bastian Harris, and Gareth Vaughan